Interpretation Third

Interpretation Third

World We Reject (A Pre-judgment Book)

Paul Tarsleh

Paul Tarsleh
Interpretation Third

Published by Spines

ISBN: 979-8-89569-788-7

Like He did in Heavens, God has been dealing with the earth in dispensations.

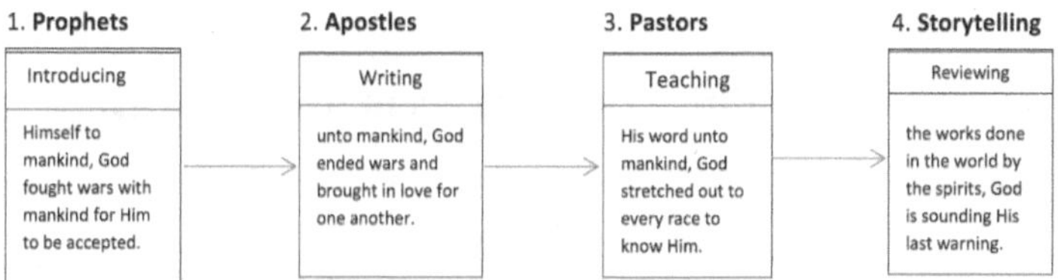

- **Time for teaching how to be righteous is over; it's quizzing and review time.** Remember that before a final exam in school, a teacher gives a quiz and a review. So, this is God's own time to quiz on what has been taught and review all that has been written. And before court action takes place, sometimes a judge gives legal advice, so this is God's own time to give His final advice.

- In this review, there are two Spiritual Truths that remain the secret things of the new world to come. God chooses to be silent on them due to some peculiar reasons.

- In this review, there is only one place previously chosen by God to be the peace center for all peoples to run to, to learn peace, but the people there have neglected peace talks and have lost their purpose in the world. God wants to defend Himself against some misunderstandings of His actions to them right now before the world. Therefore, let the world open its ears.

- Every Christian has heard about the narrow gate and how many are called, but few shall be chosen. Now is the time to define that narrow gate and how few shall be qualified among the many who're doing the work of God today.

- Every man knows how sweet the fish is, but not all know whether human poop makes the fish sweeter. This you'll know only when you open the fish's gut after it has just eaten poop. This is how the sweet things we do are made of poop [dirty things], but we don't see how dirty until now when God opens up the guts of our lives.

- Before the first world was destroyed, Noah was sent to advance God's warning. Now, I am that physical man to offer God's warning to physical men.

- Oh! See how pitiful it is to be rich and later turn poor; it's just how the world majority goes about enjoying the world in all of its riches [everything that glitters to the majority here in this world and they do every day], but the same way a majority of people shall suffer perpetual gnashing and grunting in heavenly prison while a very tiny number [like the few suffering on earth to do things right] shall rest in heavenly paradise.

These issues in this mission statement are brought to the people of the world in four major books, and this is just one of them.

Contents

Notice

This book uses 42 Bible verses in total, all from the New American Standard Bible (NASB).

The author didn't necessarily have to put in biblical quotations as he did in most parts, but for the sake of layman's doubt, he had to push in some quotations while some verses were not directly quoted but instead used as references to assure readers that what had been discussed was Bible-based.

Permission to Quote

Introduction

Many people wonder whether God exists. In some parts of the world where science floods societies with goods and comfort, the importance of God has diminished already; instead, the church is the place of employment and money-making more than a place of changing the world to a peaceful and loving place for humanity. As the people turned to science for answers to life, what to do and not to do to be healthy, to get what you need to live, God came down in December 2005 in Africa and arrested a black man to use to review his word (the Bible) and reveal some secret things of the Spirit to mankind before He destroys everything the very scientists have built on earth and are building in Space.

After the man was arrested, he was put in a school of the Spirit for two and a half years, from 2006 to mid-2008, when he listened to the voices of invisible beings (spirits/angels) who told him many things about the world's happenings.

When Spirit took me (PAUL) into the Spirit realm in 2008 at the closing of my training in the school of the Spirit, I was terrified by the colossal image I saw. It stood in the deep sea with many creatures' heads. They stood high in the sky, stretching out of the sea into the lands in all directions. Some were pouring fire from their mouths, others pouring cold, others pouring smoke, and others pouring dew. Still, I couldn't recognize everything that was coming out of others because they swiveled their heads swiftly from one direction to another.

A voice came to me and said that the large image represents a nation with many leaders pouring troubles into the lands. He said that there is so much trouble in humans' lands, but only one nation is troubling them.

The voice inspired me with many stories about the nation of troubles and commanded me to write them unto the people. These stories and related stories comprise this book.

When I heard these words, I remembered one sermon a pastor preached in the past from the book of Ezekiel. He said the book of Ezekiel was written when wickedness filled the hearts of a place called Tyre. Then, I asked myself, could this be a message to the land that is causing trouble in the land of humans? [In this story, land can be a nation and can be the entire world].

So, I asked myself another question: What's happening in the land?

In the land [world], I hear noises. There are wars; there are arguments about reforms; there are technological competitions; there are arguments about independence; there are new alliances, and there is so much going on in the land, the land of humans.

The land is in turmoil; the old and rich lands continue in their old-fashioned ways of telling everyone what to do or say, but the new alliance of nations is in protest, protesting changes in the old ways, protesting equal participation in decision making, protesting new arrangements for businesses, protesting freedom to choose new friends and do new businesses, protesting justice for all, protesting technological and infrastructural development for all humanity.

When I see this happening, I say, oh, democracy is coming back to bite its owners because I see the entire world quoting the same democratic values often demanded by those who set the systems everyone has fallen in love with.

I see a nation caught between two choices: surrender to the old mother or continue to die in a proxy war for those who want to conquer all. I see the stubbornness of one big nation bent on defending its border interest, no matter what.

Still, I see another nation the world sees on the mountaintop. It is slanderous; it uses the Bible to continue in its old way of wars; it is proud and arrogant; it is vengeful; it sees itself as the most righteous among mankind; still, it is inhumane; it teaches wars that it must fulfill by all means in the name of the Almighty God.

On the other hand, I see a nation pouring out tears unto God; the children and women are dying; they are weak under the weapons of mass destruction: breaking down the tall houses in rubbles, breaking down the schools, breaking down the hospitals, breaking everything everywhere. God hears their cries every day.

I see a nation of many heads using violent means to call for world peace, unity, love, and development. Still, they have failed in all their wisdom since they chose violence to solve the problems in the land.

I see a nation of many heads coaxing everyone through a government system. They call it democracy, but the protesters ask: Is democracy not equitable? Shouldn't it be equitable? They see injustice.

A war broke out in 2022. Before that, I heard the protest of a king of another kingdom saying that no one comes near his border because he doesn't go to others' borders. He said, let's stay in our respective areas of control, but the people on the other side said no, there are so many mineral resources near you, so we need them for our national development. So, your son, living right at your border, has those minerals and wants to give us those minerals. That's why we must give him all of the money and weapons he needs to destroy your empire; then, you won't have any border to defend anymore. Then, we can get anything from your son, even in your kingdom. So, the war is still going on; people are dying in their thousands, properties have been destroyed, and cities are going down slowly in ruins. Soon, the empire would crumble, the greedy ones would enter the kingdom to sit over everything, and they would expand their empire beyond their natural territories.

But I (PAUL) tell you this: I see that war is helping the kingdom develop its science and technology more than it started. I see that the kingdom is making more friends now than when the war started. I see that the kingdom is energized now by the arrogance of others to create more weapons and sell to many other nations that have long been trampled on. I see that the coalition of adversaries against adversaries is growing more than when the war started. I see more trouble than peace would come to many nations. So, I wonder whether the war can end soon, who can win it, or how it could end.

Still, while the war for mineral control is raging, I see other war preparations on the other side.

There was a kingdom of more people where almost everything was made. Every great nation has built factories there, using the nation's population to manufacture the goods everyone needs in the world. Companies paid less to the people, and they made profits in their home countries and around the world. But recently, the kingdom hasn't accepted everything the technological countries wanted it to do. So, the technological countries have launched an economic war against the kingdom. They wouldn't sell their high-end technologies to that kingdom anymore. They call it decoupling. It makes that country strong, but the technological countries wouldn't accept that kingdom becoming self-sufficient. That is why they are preparing for another war to break everything down in that kingdom; they think it is the only way to be in control forever. It is the only way to end alternative ideas in the rest of the world. It is the only way the world can continue to bow to one system.

But in all of this, I lament the land of the dark color. The land of the dark was once a ground for power competition, but that competition didn't allow the dark color to develop its sciences. They became complacent and relied on those powers that took over the dark-colored land. Today, the dark land is saddled with unemployment, poverty, and underdevelopment. They cannot advance because those powers wouldn't share technology with them. They wouldn't advance because they don't always make their own decisions; instead, they must consult and get approval [endorsement] from the controlling powers. They're the market ground for the powers with technology.

Once again, I see power competition in the dark-colored land. This time, it is a global power competition: the old powers are facing competition from new powers in the east, middle, central, and west of other regions of the world because from the east comes a new business model called "A win-win" that benefits all parties [call it give me what you have and I give you what I have), from the east comes science and technology that is willing to develop the dark-colored land and other lands that were left behind in infrastructural development.

So, the old powers want to prevent every East power's beneficiary from reaping development opportunities by taking the war to the East as it does in the West of the other land (Asialand) of other people with different ruling systems.

This book is based on my 2008 revelations about the land of many heads and its people. God analogized the land of many heads with the colossal image I saw standing in the deep sea.

The Spirit told me this about the people of the land with many heads in the sea: They claim that they're the best people of God on earth, yet look at the things they do. They do many things that are not of God, and they do them in the name of God. They see everyone who is against their ways as evil people. They wage wars in the name of protecting the name of God. They're printing more books in my (God's) name but changing my words to suit their desires. They're inserting their constitutional provisions into my word. They're making the rules for the world. They're commandeering [militarily compelling] everyone to bow to anything they put to pen. Everyone loves them because of the god they worship (the god of wealth who rules over the world), whom everyone needs to buy and get anything in the world. They're the image I (God) showed you standing in the sea.

When I (PAUL) heard these things, I was terrified and didn't want to write them at all, but the man of God said to me: They're proud Christians, so they must know how Jesus told people the truths about some things and people, such as when he called the woman a "dog" (*Matthew 15:26: He [Jesus] replied, "It is not good to take the children's bread and throw it to the dogs."*)

He called Peter "Satan" (*Matthew 16:23: But he turned and said to Peter, "Get behind me, Satan! You are a stumbling block to me; for you are not setting your mind on God's interest, but man's."*)

And he called the Jews "Hypocrites" ***(Matthew 23:1-12: "Then Jesus spoke to the crowds and to his disciples, [2] saying: The scribes and the Pharisees" [theologians & jurists, and Observers of the laws] "have seated themselves in the chair of Moses; [3] therefore all that they tell you, do and observe, but do not do according to their deeds; for they say things and do not do them. [4] "They tie up heavy burdens and lay them on men's shoulders; but they themselves are unwilling to move them with so***

much as a finger. [5] "But they do all their deeds to be noticed by men; for they broaden their phylacteries and lengthen the tassels of their garments, [6] "They love the place of honor at banquets and the chief seats in the synagogues, [7] and respectful greetings in the market-places, and being called Rabbi by men. [8] But do not be called Rabbi; for one is your teacher and are all brothers. [9] "Do not call anyone on earth your Father, He who is in heaven. [10] "Do not be called leaders; for one is your Leader, that is Christ. [11] "But the greatest among you shall be your servant. [12] "Whoever exalts himself shall be humbled; and whoever humbles himself shall be exalted.")

So, you see, in each event, Jesus revealed some truths about the situation he was faced with. Likewise, this book recounts things to its readers similarly to state facts about people and situations. For example, Matthew 23:12 tells us about the consequence [Abasement] of self-exaltation.

So, if I (PAUL) describe this self-exaltation in several other terms, we will have words, such as pride, ego, or pomposity. Those words would not fit the description of good biblical virtue.

Therefore, what God told me about the sea image and its peoples shall embody several descriptive terminologies that I hope should not aggravate "the people of God," for He is the God of truth.

This book, like all my other books, brings to the world detailed meaning to several biblical statements such that Christians would think that it is another man's [My, the author's] attempt to rewrite the Bible, but no, this is God's way of offering clarifications to some scriptural references that are responsible for the behaviors in Christian societies, such as the reason Christian nations, rather than pagan nations, continue to lead our world to wars as well as take the lead in the manufacturing of weapons of mass destruction, including other behaviors that will be numerated one by one in this book.

God said if Christian nations had obeyed Jesus when he told them [through Peter] to put back their swords, further saying, "No more of this," this world would have been with fewer or no wars. This world would have known love [love thy neighbor] more than the hate it perpetuates in my (God's) name.

Still, this is no attempt to stop the way the world is going now but is simply, perhaps only, to unveil the old things that have been obscured with biblical shortcuts in the form of parables all this while. In the end, everyone would choose for themselves whether to keep on going the way they're going or to stop.

This book postulates that perhaps revealing these things will help the people choose wisely how to write a new constitution for the new united world.

Also, let me say this: This book is a mirror or reflection of universal values considered acceptable norms and always imposed on the rest of the world's populace. I tell you this: God looks at them through the pinhole. That's why I call it a pre-judgment book.

Still, this book would reveal how humanity is suffering because they abandoned the world God loves but chose the wrong one God hates. Mankind has fallen in love with a government system that is responsible for greed and other habits that mankind suffers from. Greed is one of the things causing wars around the world. Still, there is another government system in our world that the majority of people reject in this world. It is the perfect way to solve humanity's problems.

Among many things revealed in this book is the amount of damage science and human rights have done to God's word and work. Science is a field of study that takes away the minds of many people from God. Human science makes the story of God turn weird in many people's ears. They don't want to hear that this world will end one day.

Many people believe in human science because it is physical, while God is Spiritual. Science creates things people can see and touch. It lays down a pattern anyone can follow to create something, but God is invisible. He cannot visibly and audibly speak to people to teach them any pattern to follow to create things. Still, He is the great architect of all the knowledge in human science.

Lastly, with all said, the author wants to let you know one thing as you prepare to go into this book.

He's not writing to make the world perfect; rather, he's writing on behalf of God, who wants to point out where the world has strayed from the right things.

In my home country-Liberia

In my other two books, *Interpretation First* and *Interpretation Second,* I revealed the three primary human colors God created. Each of these has its own internal variations, which is why every race has different skin pigmentations.

Also, I revealed how one human color has dominated the world with its fast-growing knowledge of everything it touches. The books I read in primary school told me things about this race, but in my country, I have never seen anyone from that race.

The first white man I have ever seen

As a little boy coming up, I did not know of any other human color until I saw Yenplu Toe in Geekan.

I later learned he was a Canadian whose official name was "James Large." However, all sparkling clean skin color people are called "white people" in my home country. So, I don't know how Europeans determined themselves alone to be white because their skin color is the same as Canadians, Mexicans, Russians, and even the Chinese have sparkling clean skin color people, except for the hair textures and other features.

He came to my home country, Liberia, to study Liberian culture, but he chose to study the Grebo culture, which is the tribe that I hail from.

The story about Yenplu Toe was told by my grandfather the first time he took me to Geekan, a little town where Yenplu Toe lives, where I saw that different color of a man among the black/dark skins.

My grandfather said that when that color of a man got to the Grebo people, called Chedepo people, he chose to settle among them and go away from the car road, but not to go too far away to shorten his walking distance. So, he decided to find a nearby village, and that's how he came to Geekan. I think it's about a one-hour and a half walk from the national highway, a highway from the Capital, Monrovia, and passes through my maternal hometown called "Putuken" and leads to Maryland County, the home of Liberia's longest-serving President- President William V. S. Tubman.

As is customary by all strangers who want to settle down among the people, in Geekan, the white man chose to be a member of a particular household group that he could always refer to as his family. So, he asked for a native name that would give him total belonging, which made the kinsmen in his family give him the name "Toe." But, according to my grandfather, whose paternal root comes from this Geekan, there was always a question of which Toe whenever the name came up in any discussion in the village/town. So, to distinguish him from the black Toes, they added a descriptive title as "White" before the Toe, thus earning him a play name as Yenplu Toe, translated as "White person Toe."

Yenplu Toe (James Large) then learned how to speak the Chedepo dialect and became very fluent in it, so much so that he embarked on crafting a writing work on it. Eventually, phonic works were produced, so now, there is a Chedepo dialect book available in the Bible.

Unfortunately, few people, including myself, have learned to write our local language using those phonics.

There is a reluctance to study how to coin together our own words so that we can make sentences and communicate with one another through writing. This reluctance stems from the fact that this work of phonetic writing came late to us.

After all, our society has opened up to traveling far away to different parts of the country and the world, and the only language that is required to communicate effectively with people from different places is the English language, which belongs to the white man. In fact, our fathers and grandees have started learning English; even though they spoke in broken tongues, they desired to do better than they talked. This made it less essential to sit in class to learn how to craft together words that would not go across borders.

Yet I speak my local language, but I cannot write it.

The Missionaries

The second time I had seen a white color human being was a group of white people labeled as "Missionaries." These were a group of Church workers who came to my hometown as teachers of monotheism – serving one God system.

They went from house to house and from one tiny village to another to teach the Bible. They often came to the branch of the Assembly of God Church (AG Church) in Putuken, established by a son of the town named Rev. Jeddi.

These people taught obedience to God and abstinence from sins. They condemned the ways of our people, such as polygamy, drunkenness, sexual immorality, and the rest you know.

The Peace Corps

The Liberian government school system received a group of Americans labeled "Peace Corps" or "Peace Corps Volunteers." They were posted to various schools throughout Liberia. According to my older cousins, who these white people taught, our hometown initially received two or three of them in Elementary and Junior High school in the early '70s.

These Peace Corps also carried the Bible with them so they could teach students how to say the Lord's Prayer every morning during devotion time. They also taught Christian songs.

Seeing all this, it was difficult for me to think that there was any unbeliever in the Western world, especially the US.

So, from their teachings, the first glimpse of life that I had of the white people (American people) was that their country was very law-abiding to the ordinances of God.

Though naïve I was to think that they were all pure in hearts, I believed that at least the majority were very obedient to God.

But later, I learned that a tiny number of people thrive on obedience to the Bible, which they print, preach, and teach everywhere.

This I'm talking about is going to be laid out to you throughout several chapters of this book to make it easier for you to agree with me. I will use the Bible to help you understand that they deviated from the Bible long ago.

As I conclude this white human story of teaching the Bible to us, I can't stop reflecting on the image God showed me standing in the sea. I'm confused whether it represents America and its people. However, since I'm currently living in the US and have seen some things here, allow me to discuss what I see happening here and around the world through the power [ways of life] of the Americans.

Still, I think God raised me to give the Americans His message that also goes to all those who take pleasure in their (American) lifestyles. I think He wants me to do this even before His judgment comes upon our land—the world.

How they overwhelmed our system

Though the Peace Corps worked with our school system, our school textbooks did not entirely reflect American stories; rather, they were more based on European stories.

This was more vivid from the literature books that contained stories like "The Wing Horse/Pegasus."

In 1st, 2nd, and 3rd grade, I did not cease to laugh every time my literature teacher, Mrs. Saydee, but we called her "Ma Elizabeth," came to class for us to read a story titled "Little Man in The Red Jacket."

From a little man's point of view, this main character in the story seemed to be stupid to us since we did not initially comprehend why he kept chasing after a strange nose that kept growing and growing. This kept the entire class laughing at him each day we took turns to read. Still, the indisputable fact was that he was adventurous and curious to know where the nose would end up and what the nose was searching for, or better still, why the nose was growing. And as the story ended, he discovered gold treasures. This one may have been an American gold story, but the setting has slipped my mind since my elementary days.

From another story, the title of which I have forgotten, I fell in love with the name 'Douglas' used for one other character, Douglas Wilson. I loved the name so much that I wanted to change my name to Douglas, but I was not privileged to do so since my parents insisted that I use the name given at birth, which bore meaning to circumstances they knew. Unfortunately, I changed my native name and assumed the English name "Paul," which I was told my biological father gave me since he loved God.

Reflecting on the past now, I can say that white people's stories dominated our learning capacity more than we studied about ourselves. This takes me back to what I said earlier: learning our own local phonics, including reading folktales about ourselves, became less important to our [my] growing up. So, the mix of European and American textbooks in our schools made me think that the white man's cultural stories overwhelmed our lands.

This is the beginning of White's superficial superiority.

But from my junior high school years, I learned that America's relationship with my country and the world at large dominated all other white countries. This became clearer when I moved to the Capital City-Monrovia in 1983.

In Monrovia, I went to watch American Cable News in the USAID Library, located near the US Embassy in Mamba Point, Monrovia-Liberia.

By 1985, when I got to 9th grade, my going there was no longer about watching American News about US President Ronald Reagan and Russian President Mikhail Gorbachev over nuclear issues, but was also for research in world history about World War I & II, emphasized by the heroism of the American people who dropped the atomic bomb on the Japanese Islands of Hiroshima Nagasaki.

The American government and its people were involved in every sector of my country's government's operations, directing and training them on what and how to run their own government. They also gave financial aid.

The Americans were also heard of in every African country, giving aid, offering critical analyses of every government function, charging government officials with corruption and malpractices, and calling for investigations and prosecutions.

They taught and preached human rights every day, and through these teachings and preaching, they exported their cultural behaviors into every corner of Africa. Among them are their ways of dressing, celebrating, eating, treating women and children, and making love.

Their money is a god above any nation's own currency.

I realized later that they threw money into African countries in the same way they did and still do in every country in the world. In my home country, this creates a high desire in young people to go to the US.

So, some young people came to the US through government scholarships, and others came through other programs. My eldest brother was among them.

While they stayed abroad, they sent pictures home that showed how healthy and good-looking they were. They showed the kind of cars they drove, the parties they attended, and the nightclubs they went to. All of these sent good signals back home that in America, all is well *[The US is viewed as the paradise on earth {God's beautiful city with no suffering}].*

When some of them visited home periodically, they threw fabulous parties and gave money, or what our people called "large amounts of money," to relatives and friends.

And when you look at someone like that who was once a peasant in Liberia, we say "a common farmer," who didn't own a bedroom house [since zinc was expensive to buy so our people would say "one who never owned a zinc house"], but now owns one and drives a car in America, all that comes to everyone's mind is to take up wings to fly over the sea and drop down in America, without any idea as to what would happen to him if he flew and dropped down in the streets of America.

That was how I used to dream of coming to the US whenever one of my countrymen visited home from the US in the 80s, but my brother never visited.

My dreams about the US

I have twelve siblings alive, two sisters and ten boys, but only seven of us boys interacted together as we were growing up after our father was assassinated in 1974.

Every day, as we walked through bush paths to farmlands, we talked about our eldest brother coming so that we could be with him in the US one day. This was all we dreamed about everywhere we found ourselves, and it always gave us the strength to stick together. However, I didn't know him, except by photos.

The first time I ever received money from him was in 1989 when I was about to graduate from High School. It was USD 50.00.

He gave us all one condition: He would sponsor the person who won the US Diversity Visa (DV) Lottery to come to the US.

I did not play until 2000 for DV2001, and I was one of the few who won it that year.

However, I did not get the promised support and had to forfeit the opportunity.

Then, I got a procurement job at an Iron Ore mining company, ArcelorMittal-Liberia, in 2010.

It was my first-lifetime opportunity to have a job with a net salary of USD 456.00 at an exchange rate of 60 Liberian Dollars (LD), or $27,360 monthly. However, I was not content with the job because of some practices that were incompatible with my inner self. Even while I made extra money through the system I hated, I still yearned for America, where I had no imagination that something like corruption, favoritism, or even hard labor existed at all.

Fortunately for me, the time arrived in 2013 when I obtained a US visiting business visa because I had just published my first two books and was invited by the publishing firm AuthorHouse, UK, to attend a Book Signing event in Miami, Florida.

When I first arrived in November of that year, it was a dream come true. After the event, I returned home in December 2013.

I lodged with my kid sister in Atlanta, Georgia. A week before Thanksgiving, my brother-in-law drove me to Florida in a rental car.

While we drove through the highway to Florida for more than six hours, I began to admire the sceneries of a clean environment, pavement everywhere, food shops along the route, and a lot that my country lacks, especially the spaghetti road system (The many crisscrossing of roads) that I saw while entering the city of Miami.

But I had a first-time shocking experience of America's system.

On our way from Atlanta, we searched online for hotel lodging, and we found one in the nearby city of Fort Lauderdale for a reasonable price. Everything appeared excellent in the picture online: nice building, nice rooms, nice beds and sheets, excellent food, and the talk about good customer service.

But my brother-in-law and I did not sleep well that night. We were bitten throughout that night by bedbugs that we did not recognize early. In fact, the mere thought of seeing bedbugs in US hotels was far unimaginable, and that made it take us so long to see that there were bedbugs in our twin beds.

In the morning, we had to practically beg for our breakfast before leaving for the event in Miami.

Gosh, what a place! Can you imagine that a place like this exists in the US? Now, the question that popped into my mind was, where is the US government that checks everything people do in other countries?

This was my first assessment of a bad system in the US, but I would discover more in the following years.

Now I can see things in the US

I had a one-year visa that was still open until December 2014, so I took leave in August 2014 to revisit the US, hoping to explore some opportunities to find partners or sponsors for my books. You know, I didn't know much about how the book business works, so I thought it was easy to go about it once you had something good to tell, but little did I know how Herculean it is.

The first week I arrived was the same week a Liberian named Duncan arrived in the US with the Ebola virus from West Africa.

Gosh!!! Americans became irritant towards Africans, particularly those from West Africa, where the Ebola virus was raging havoc in Guinea, Sierra Leone, and Liberia. People became scared of us, the new arrivals from West Africa, charging us with being carriers of the virus, and the US government warned citizens not to go close to us.

West Africa then became a no-go zone, so we were

stranded from returning to a virus-infested place. Companies were shutting down, including ArcelorMittal-Liberia, which downsized its employees and scaled back production.

So, I stayed back in the US to find a new way to restart my life after I had overstayed my leave.

Facing society's *Language issue*

Living in the US is a difficult thing that begins with language issues.

I was happy to see myself in the US, but I was shamed every day for the way I spoke, the sounds I made, and the English words I used.

Wherever I went and whenever I spoke to someone, the first statement that I heard was "Excuse me" or "Say that again," and the next one was the question, "Where do you come from?"

Oh gosh, this "*Say that again*" and that "*Where you come from?*" have never ceased to embarrass me all the time, even up to now, but it is kind of better this time. In fact, the thought of someone asking me '*where you come from*' whenever I wanted to speak to an American made me scared to try to engage in a conversation with anyone.

It got worse whenever I went to buy something. In a grocery store, one time, I asked for the aisle where I could find what we call "Butter Pear" in Liberia, but no one knew what I was talking about. Still, I was asking about "Avocado" in the US. This is how I got confused about the origin of the words we learned from the books we used in schools, which were written by English people and sent from Europe or the

US. So, I pondered how Americans didn't know what a butter pear was.

But on their part, too, one thing that sounded—and still sounds—awful to my ears is the word 'Anyway,' which is often pronounced and spelled "Anyways" in America.

Throughout my English class, I never saw an 's' to the adverb 'Anyway,' which stands for 'in any case,' 'however,' 'regardless,' 'in any event,' etc.

So, while they laughed at me for how I pronounced some English words, I also laughed at them for using the wrong English words. Even in writing, I see so many errors that I never thought could be made by white Americans.

Work issue

My second shock. My job in 2015 at Walgreens Distribution Center in Woodland, California, was really my second job in the US. I worked there for just one month and then left due to a broken ankle outside the job.

I worked in the warehouse receiving and shipping department. Gosh, what a hard laborer job! As a receiver, you had the duty to grab the boxes at the fastest pace that rolled on an electric belt. Otherwise, the belt would stop rolling because you would cause the loads to jam together, which would prevent the belt from rolling freely.

Some of these boxes are heavy, while some are lighter, but there is no easy way to tell which is lighter or heavier because some smaller boxes contain lithium items, which are heavier than most items.

So, if you are not careful enough, you may spring your back before you know it.

Another thing: You're grabbing the boxes, setting them on the floor, and packing them on a pallet. You are not only packing them on the pallet, but you must arrange them properly to be more than five feet high.

The job's annoying part is that smaller and larger boxes are fitted together on a pallet and must be arranged appropriately. This usually causes them to collapse, which will cause you to start packing them on a pallet all over again, even while you continue grabbing new arrivals from the belt.

Any day you were assigned a truck for loading, your trouble is bigger because here, you lift and throw the boxes into the air to fill the upper level far above your reach until the whole truck is fully loaded.

Therefore, you must be someone who goes to the gym to practice heavy weightlifting. To do such work, you must learn to work at the pace of a robot.

Wow, seriously, does this kind of job exist in the US? This is not what people in Liberia think work looks like in the US. We believe that machines do all the heavy lifting. We think that people do not sweat so much when working in the US. So, I was so disappointed to do this kind of job, especially since I came from a white-collar job, a procurement officer sitting in an air-conditioned office using a computer to source goods to buy for the company.

Wage issue

Oops, my whole heart was left disappointed when I realized how much my take-home pay would be for my eight-hour-a-day job. It wouldn't cover my rent alone after taking out my gas and lunches for the month. Let's see the table below.

Wage calculation						
Hours	Rate	Daily wage	Days in week	Weekly wage	Weeks in month	Monthly gross income
8	$13.65	**$109.2**	5	$546	4	**$2,184**

That's how my gross earnings should have looked before taxes. It means my net earnings were due to be less than $2,000.

Every Liberian back home who has never been to the US and has heard about this amount would think that this is a lot of money, but no, this was far from taking care of my needs in the US.

I was living with a woman already, my fiancé then but now my wife. She would tell me how much I needed to contribute to keep up the house. I also had to save towards the renewal of my Temporary Protected Status (TPS) that was issued for six months and put some savings towards marriage and another savings to prepare to file for a Green Card whenever the time comes. I was also required to buy lunch for work and gas every month for the car she bought for me. Don't forget that I left six children in Africa to cater to. They listen at the end of every month to hear phone calls where Daddy would say, hey, get a pen and paper to write down this Western Union or MoneyGram number. Still, there was another need to save money to publish new books or market the books I had written already, which were lying down for lack of funds. All these did not fit in the budget for, let's say, $1,460 as net income [not sure how much the net income was since I lost the pay stub before writing this book].

The need for a second job

Now, my fiancé would say get a second job, but I couldn't because I work a graveyard shift where I don't sleep until 5:00 AM to clock out and reach home by 5:45/6:00 AM. When I come home, I need to rest for some hours, which makes it impossible for me to get another job starting at 6/7/8 AM and ending at 12/1/2 PM. It was also impossible for me to get any job that starts at 2:00 PM and ends at 10:00 PM since my graveyard job starts at 10:00 PM. It was challenging to get one to augment my Walgreens salary.

When my ankle healed, I began doing Temporary jobs with Temp Agencies for $12.00 or $13.00. However, they were all hard laborer jobs like the Walgreens job, so my back began to ache, and I couldn't stop complaining.

The pressure to earn more was so much that I had no peace. I began to think about whether I could make it successfully in the US. If I could, then how?

The kinds of jobs in the US

My fiancé works as a Certified Nursing Assistant (C.N.A.) in a facility. She also works with an In-Home service provider agency as a Personal Attendant; other areas call it a caregiver. These jobs make her bring home up to $4,000+ or $5,000+ some months. So, she kept encouraging me to join her for the In-Home services since the warehouse jobs were giving me back pain.

Initially, I felt nasty about it since it involved doing personal hygiene and bathing people with disabilities. Still, later, I gave in to her advice because I wanted to save myself for the old age time and to enable me to work multiple shifts to earn more. In fact, it was comparably time allowing to do, so she stayed three to four days working out there before coming home, and it made her earn more even at the pay rate of $11.00, $12.00 & $13.00, then $14.00 by the time of starting this book in December 2020.

So, I got an In-Home service job where I work regular hours of 316 per month at the rate of $14.00/Hour. With this pay rate and many hours, I can now breathe a little easier since my rent and car note are fully covered, and I have a little left for other things.

This has enabled me to cover the costs of publishing my first three books in the US in 2020. The titles have been changed during the 2024 republished versions.

However, the issue of low wages, causing people who wallop in poverty in the US to [must] work two or more jobs or multiple shifts, is a problem with capitalism. That problem is what I'll be expanding on in another topic concerning the two opposing government systems that are in the world right now. Also, God spoke much about what capitalism is doing against world peace.

But before going there, let me tell you what happens to people like me and my wife who work these many hours or have to work more than one job or shift.

We work these long hours at low pay rates because we never sleep at home in the three-bedroom house of $3,145.14 (mortgage, bills, and others) throughout each month. My wife and I don't ever sleep together throughout the year since she has to sleep at clients' homes just as I do, and when one person has the chance to rest at home for whatever emergency reason, the next person would still be at work.

Americans' Work Habit

I would also love to explain this more under another topic concerning capitalism and communalism or democratic and communist practices.

I would say that Americans don't like to work. People are working because they're compelled to do so by the system to make a living.

During my temp job, I worked with a cross-section of people who would not like to do their jobs perfectly, except there was an eye on them every ten to fifteen minutes.

When I was at Kokeva, in Roseville, California, where we had to pack repaired electronic items on pallets for shipment or receive new ones for shelving, I wouldn't stop doing something even when my supervisor was never around, but my fellow co-workers would linger around, pretending to be doing something on the computer or the floor once our supervisor was out of sight. The work was there to do, but they said I didn't have to work so much once there was no specific target to chase each day.

They began to stereotype me as an African bushman who was used to working in the farm fields.

This attitude was typical among Black Americans and some white Americans who usually said America is their home and they can do whatever they want, including getting another job anytime and anywhere.

The habit of paying more attention to the job was common among the immigrant community, mainly Africans, Mexicans, and Asians.

The habit of don't-like-to-work was less visible until I got into the In-Home service job. Here, the job description called for many things, including doing house chores while working with a client (a person with disabilities) to help him/her achieve some level of independence. To help him/her achieve some level of independence means to allow him/her to do some house chores or cooking in any way possible that he/she could.

The Employment Manual states that failure to do these things or take care of the client would amount to neglect of the client.

However, I got so irritated and always disappointed at the attitudes of most co-workers who went to work and chose to spend more than 80% of their time on phones, using social media, listening to music, or watching movies without attending to the client's needs. Using the phone can be done without neglecting duties.

This made me angry at one of my client's homes, which made me take pictures of how she was neglected despite my mandatory reporting (See something, say something) to our supervisor. Please see the following two images:

A

The staff bought her own food and ate at the client's house, but the staff didn't wash the bowl or trash it after eating.

So, leaving everything there was passing her mess over to the next staff.

B

The staff prompted the client to do her chores/dishes, but the client didn't have the ability to do a clean job each time she was encouraged to wash her own dishes.

In this case, the job requires the staff to assist the client, but, here, the staff left the client's dishes messy as seen above.

What was habitual was their constant refusal to do some of the basic things for which they were employed, such as sweeping, laundering, washing dishes, or bathing the client.

I always asked the question: Why did they seek employment when they were not ready or willing to do the job?

I was always angry to see them paid their full salary at the end of every month when, in fact, they did not do their jobs properly but rather left them for me, just the same way my wife would complain about her workplace, too.

So, whenever my wife complained to me, as I did almost

every day, and we shared our frustrations together on the phone, the only thing that I said to her was that it would have been better if our world had adopted a system in which every man didn't have to work so many hours to get paid before earning a living because that's what Americans want—to sit down and do less or nothing to get paid for making a living.

Almost all work-before-get-paid Americans very welcomed this sit-down-to-do-nothing-and-get-paid system during the COVID-19 pandemic crisis, when the US government ditched out free money to every citizen, either as an individual or a business entity, due to the sit-at-home order that the pandemic brought upon the nation. This order shut down almost every business or workplace, thus throwing people out of jobs.

A lot of people filed for unemployment money. I bet they would have loved to continue receiving that kind of money forever, should the pandemic persist longer, or the government choose to continue giving free money to people to live their lives- sleep, eat, drink, smoke, make love, and go back to sleep for the next day.

Love making issue

As I said earlier in Chapter One, under discussion about American missionaries in Liberia, sexual immorality was condemned vehemently in Liberia/Africa.

The missionaries taught in churches that having many wives or making love here and there was very immoral and that God hates it and it's a sin. Although I came from a polygamous background and I probably have that ugly seed in me, I still felt guilty about being with several women. Still, this guilt kept me looking for the right way while investigating the reasons the US continues to promote sexual immorality to the highest order in the world.

While I was in Africa and saw great preachers like Jimmy Swagger and Billy Graham and donations of Bibles from American churches, all I thought about was that the many Bibles they print, teach, and preach all over the world would make this nation a perfect society or at least less immoral.

The Bibles are the same they use to judge others around the world. But as I sit somewhere in the corner of Foothills, near Elkhorn Blvd, Sacramento, California, USA, to write this book, I'm so disappointed to learn that monogamy is not honorable in the US and that promiscuity is the most common practice. This is a fact, even if you refuse to acknowledge it.

Even though the US government acts like it has respect for marriage and that adultery is illegal, the same government gives licenses for prostitution and enacts laws that permit other sexual acts. And it is an open secret on the internet where people talk about open marriage, hook-up, one-night stands, and the rest that defines a society that takes pleasure in everything about sex that God hates.

It makes me question the purpose of the Bible they adorn so much. Isn't it the purpose that the Bible reduces crimes in the world, which the Bible defines as "Striving towards perfection?" So, why would a nation that boasts about calling itself the best God's nation promote those human practices God frowns on by granting licenses and enacting laws to guarantee these acts more than enacting laws to curb/suppress them?

> Please let me deliver to you God's message handed down to me in 2008 concerning nations' laws.
>
> He said, He did not inspire the Bible to say that there wouldn't be sinners among the people of God, neither would there not be backsliders from the believers, nor say that all the people would be 100% perfect, but that when a nation enacts laws that legally allow its people to practice wrong acts; that nation has purposely [intentionally] endorsed the promotion of wrongful living. He said the laws that should serve as deterrence have therefore become impetus to any wrongful practice.
>
> He said, any nation found enacting laws that tells its citizens that they can do whatever they like regardless of what the Bible says about it, that nation is no better than a nation of sins, and that such nation is like Sodom and Gomorrah where sins were part of the daily living of the people and that they abandoned the laws of God.
>
> He said even though there were a few faithful in Sodom and Gomorrah, He deemed those nations sinners who deserved to be destroyed, and they were destroyed.

So, it is against the boast of the US nation that this book comes about to present a numeration of the things they do in the world and is to give them a mirror to look in before the end comes. Therefore, this book is primarily based on Americans' ways of life to reflect that God is showing mankind the wrongs of the world by using the one nation that leads all the world's peoples. It is a nation that has all the lifestyles that every nation now emulates everywhere nowadays.

Marriage issue

In my Interpretation First book, I discussed marriage extensively, starting with how it came about and why God initially endorsed it. Then, I contrasted it with marriage today. I want to refer you to that book.

But let's reflect: Marriage is based on the principle of one-to-one forever. So, how can it be an open practice that allows each person to do what God wants to prevent? [Check the *Interpretation First* book]. So, if there should be such things as "open marriage," then why should people marry?

Other problems in America

While I was in my home country, I heard the news about racism (The divide between blacks and whites in the US), but now I'm here, and I have seen several other segregations. So, through me, God, who told me to come to the Western world before writing this book, wants to address the issue. But before I go into that, let me deliver God's message.

God explained to me the parable of the man who planted good seeds and the other man who went at night to plant weeds amongst the master's seeds.

He said He made everything good, and He made us human beings to be one, but the divisions we have amongst ourselves in this world are from another Kingdom. So, to get a full story of how these divisions started, please find my other book titled, *Interpretation First*, which explains the activities of the gods of our lands.

To understand that that division is not from God, let's look at the oneness He created for us all.

When we are born into this world, we all are babies that speak one language. I mean to say all babies cry or talk the same, regardless of color or geographical origin. It is while we are in this world that we begin to learn the togues of our parents or whichever language that surrounds us.

When we become grownups and start to make love, we use only one entry method. No matter what color background we come from, the idea of love making means one thing between a woman and a man.

We all also share one color of blood [red], one water kind of tears, one way of grief or shedding tears, one way we lie down to sleep, and many other things that do not change at all, no matter where one comes from.

These are the things making us one people and should make us not to distinguish, but the opposite exists in our world somehow.

To begin the discussion on racism, I wouldn't want to use any dictionary meaning here because there would be two or more ways to discuss it. Instead, I'll say racism is the way one color or group of people looks at another color or group. In the US, it is the way white color people look at black color people, so it is an identity issue.

Since it is an identity issue, then what is identity?

This time, I went to the Google dictionary and found four different definitions, but I took definition two for this discussion.

Definition two says, "*A close similarity or affinity,*" and it has several synonyms, but two I love are "*Sameness, oneness.*" Can you see now how one color of people sees themselves as the same or one?

This is a natural tendency planted in every person, regardless of color.

How is it a natural thing for all people? Go to my Interpretation First book again to read about how Satan often tampers with every Life-given soul before it is born into this world.

To further understand this natural way of segregating/favoring others, I have adopted the table below as a pyramid to explain our typical selves.

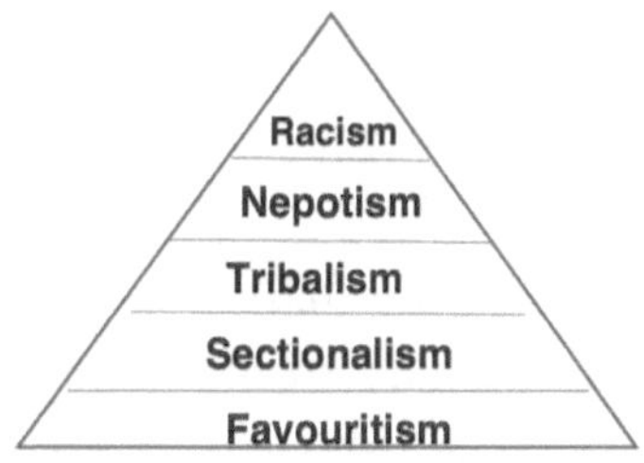

Racism – This I see as color, belongingness, or identity.

To me, it means that identifying one's color seems to be at the top of the pyramid. Starting from the bottom to the top of the pyramid, it occupies a small portion at the top of all the problems we have with belongingness. It is a choice between only two colors, a small fraction of humankind, but it's between two races.

Nepotism – I see nepotism as a practice of choosing one's relative over others. It is a practice of segregation among a small number of people, too, that makes it come second to racism.

Let's see something: A president came to power in the US where he abused the old norms of Americanism, which I called American nepotism that was common among them, but they had their way of doing it. His children were not disguised under multinational corporations, but they were right with him in his government.

In other countries, nepotism is easy to detect because it is made visible to the public. In America, I see it as a way for influential people to influence their relatives' employment over others in different work institutions.

I see it in America as a brand name to ride on to success, and it helps marginalize some people so that the wealthy continue to be wealthy and the powerful continue to be powerful.

I also see it in America as what makes the Rockefellers, the Lincolns, the Washingtons, the Bushes, the Clintons, the Gates, the Trumps, and the growing Obamas, as well as every minister, CEO, etc., continue getting lucrative jobs wherever they present themselves because phone calls are often made for ascertainment, or favors are expected in return.

Nepotism, therefore, is a privilege accorded to people because of their blood connections. It may be direct or indirect when one's relative grants favor to him/her over others or when a relative receives favor over others because of his/her relative's status in society.

But this time, God said the president who changed US norms was allowed by God to take the presidency so that He (God) would expose what Americans have been doing secretly with other people, even while they condemned others for doing those same things.

That president set America on the path of global decline. The policies he established initiated the wake-up call to other countries to seek total independence and self-sufficiency. It set the world on a new path of no return to the so-say all by America, and the world followed. His bold actions on America first have galvanized a global call for a new world order.

The mystery of God behind all this is hidden, but intelligent people would be able to see it with the advent of the voice of God from Africa. God raised His voice from Africa to tell the stories of what was happening in the lands. This book is one of the voices of Africa.

Tribalism is also a choice-making decision that runs among one color group of humankind in one nation. While racism is an international issue, tribalism is a national problem.

See the faces of two or more tribal people glow with smiles and loud waves of laughter when they meet to discover that they originate from one language group.

This discovery often enhances the friendship between two or more people who may have found themselves amongst people from different colors, countries, tribes, or even communities.

This tribal discovery may serve as a bad precedent for influencing one person's ability to give rewards, especially during employment.

Sectionalism – This is like tribalism but is a narrow way of segmenting the people of the same tribe.

Once the two or more tribal people begin to dig deeper into which town/village each came from, they attempt to sectionalize themselves. That is, though five or more of us are of the same tribe, we are not from the same town/village.

Further, dividing one tribal group into tribal segments [sections of a particular tribe] has an influence on each person's mind. In any instance where more than two persons were introducing themselves, and it is discovered that there are two among them who come from the same town/village, the two may sneak into a corner later to continue a separate conversation about their town/village, which includes finding out each person's household family name, father's and mother's names, siblings' names and on and on. This kind of information helps bond them further than they would love to be with other members of the same tribal group.

In the US, I see sectionalism as the thing that bonds black Americans and white Americans together against black Africans. It is how black Americans see themselves as more Americans than black Africans who just came or obtained American citizenship.

The way black Americans identify with white Americans [I think] stems from the fact that the forefathers and mothers of both white Americans and black Americans have lived together in the US and possibly in the same states and communities. Though they may have been divided, the fact remains that they were born and raised together, say in Ohio, so they can speak and understand the same jargon used in Ohio.

Now, I want you to see what I said earlier that the first problem an immigrant faces upon arrival in the US is language. I was talking about this segregation that black Africans receive from their fellow blacks who are branded as Negroes in the US.

Though black Americans (Negroes) make noise about racial segregation every day in the US, they also segregate black Africans. Despite a black African obtaining citizenship in the US, black Americans (Negroes) say black Africans are not more Americans than they, Negroes, are.

Their attitudes start from shunning away from black Africans whose speaking sounds do not align with the American way of pronouncing words and making the kind of inflections (rise and fall) in words and sentences they know. They go on by saying that black Africans are taking away jobs from them.

They consider themselves as not Africans at all. I have been in the company of a few of them who argue that they are black Jews who came from Egypt, which is another topic that I addressed in my other book titled '*Interpretation Second,*' which God inspired to address black origin and black retardation.

So, while they make noise about white treatment towards them - Negroes, I'm raising the voice of the black Africans who are also treated with disdain by them - Negroes.

In my Interpretation Second book, I connect Africa's failure to develop to Negroes' inability to recognize Africa as their home to which they needed to take all the things they had learned from their masters during slavery, unlike what the Israelites were able to do by taking to their promised land the things- knowledge, and material wealth, they acquired from their home of servitude.

Favoritism—I see favoritism as the broadest form of preferring one person over others. I placed it at the pyramid's base to indicate that it is the most extensive cycle of people exchanging favors.

Favoritism extends beyond giving attention to relatives and tribal groups alone but includes all social groups one might find himself/herself in, such as church groups, sporting groups, workplace groups, gym place groups, school groups, and so on.

So, do you see how we all have been practicing segregation in small and large ways and are guilty of it all?

But the reason segregation between white and black human colors in America is so loud in the News is that it goes with [I think] pomposity and stigmatization. ***Pomposity*** – is that feeling of superiority [I believe] white community share together when they meet to discuss how the country came about. When they meet, [I believe in myself that] they have stories to share that bear similarity to treatments meted against blacks during slavery. [I also think] they may have histories of the origin of their wealth. ***Stigmatization*** – on the other hand, [I believe] is that hurting feeling that the black community shares together when they meet to discuss how they survived slavery. [I believe in myself that] this feeling makes them feel inhumane in the sight of white men. It triggers them to anger every time a white person approaches them with particular questions, like in the case of a white police officer stopping and asking for a driver's license, which I don't think would be a major issue if another black person is the officer.

If I'm correct with the use of these two words – pomposity and stigmatization, then the presence of these two opposing spirits, the forces that control the powers behind the words in the two human beings of two colors, made it dangerous for the two to co-exist. These feelings create a cat-and-rat approach system between the two human colors, whereas each person walks around with a certain perception about the other - one acts like a cat that could subdue, and the other acts like a rat fearing to be subdued.

But God has this message to give to the white supremacy group, and He says violence is the highest form of segregation, for it leads to the shedding of blood. He also has this to say to the Black Lives Matter group, and He says tolerance and nonviolence are a pill for pain, for everyone loves himself/herself more in the world that Satan controls.

God said Satan needs blood, so those who yield to his knocking on the hearts make ready Satan's meals. (Truly, five people died in the January 6, 2021, Capitol attack in the US, and Satan was fed.)

> The message to both White Supremacy group and Black Lives Matter group was written in this book in December 2020 before the January 6, 2021, US Capitol attack occurred, which means that God had delivered this message in advance, but it was not delivered to the American people due to the lack of money to publish this book as quickly as other writers did.
>
> This is to tell you the authenticity of the words in this book.

Politics and Big Money

The way politics and big money are intertwined in the US plays a big role in the country's hegemony over other countries in the world. So, I'd like to explain this more in another section of this book concerning the cons of capitalism.

But it is good to note that citizens of the US suffer at the hands of these two powers more than they feel or believe they are enjoying life. For example, private entities giving millions of dollars to the government each election year are businesses that continue to exploit the country's citizens, who are often priced high for goods or services they buy from the companies. In contrast, the government rewards companies with favorable business conditions regarding how to price goods and pay wages to citizens.

In places where I worked in 2019, where I earned $13.00/Hour, I laughed at my co-workers who rejoiced when the government promised a minimum wage of $15.00 as a salary increment for low-wage earners.

They said the government was doing better, but I told them the announcement was nothing to rejoice about. I said that because while the government was telling employers to increase wages, employers were threatening to increase community prices at the same time or cut some jobs.

Though I do not have every statistic available to check which item/s has/have undergone price increment since 2018, I can quickly point to the rental cost and fluctuating gasoline prices. For example, my wife and I once lived in a three-bed-two-bath house from December 2015 to February 2022 at the author's review time. Our rent has undergone three increments: $50.00/2017, $60.00/2021, and $130/2022.

Conversely, gasoline at Arco, one of the cheapest areas in Sacramento, also changed from $2.69 to $4.45 between 2018 and 2021.

I can also remember when one of our utility companies wrote to us about a "Slight increase in cost."

Suppose we were able to identify other essential items or services out there that have undergone "slight increments" in prices either by seasons or for whatever reason. In that case, I'd be thinking about how much impact the $2.00 increments from $12.00 to $14.00 have made in our lives. When will we ever rise above the poverty level? It's the same cycle—the rich remain rich, and the poor remain poor.

I also know that whatever money every businessperson gives to the government or to "charity" has long been embedded in the company's pricing strategy and collected over a certain period, which means all of it has never been paid out. See the chart below.

Sample of pricing strategy
(Everything not included)

Any item of goods						
Cost of product	% Transportation	% Overhead (Includes taxes, fuel, etc.)	% Wages	% Spoilage	% Others (Discount, etc.)	Total sale price
$2.00	$0.80	$1.50	$1.00	$0.40	$1.50	$7.20

Two things that keep money piling up in the company's coffers are spoilage and discount.

Percent of spoilage - is a certain amount, no matter how small, added to every good's cost. It is intended to pay for any damaged item by breaking, spilling, bending, or any other way that renders it not sellable. But how many of the ten thousand pieces of "Jif Peanut butter" get damaged all the time? The answer is no. Not every day does every order of Jif Peanut butter get damaged, but the percentage remains in the price that buyers pay every time.

Percent discount - is one form of inducement that businesspeople offer customers, but before I go into details, please let me ask this question. Do you seriously think a businessperson can give out money freely to all his/her customers? Well, I'm sorry to let you know that it is impossible. No businessperson gives out money freely to his/her hundreds, thousands, or millions of customers. So, no business entity in the world spends millions of dollars buying goods to offer freely to all its customers. It's a myth.

Now, let's continue: There are many ways businesspeople induce (Encourage/attract) customers to always come back to buy from them, so let's look at only two forms of inducement.

1. Some businesspeople tell their customers that they can get the item at a reduced price. For example, if the selling price is $5.00, the customer can get $1.50 off it to pay $3.50.

2. And other businesspeople would say buy 2 and get 1 free.

Either way, the cost has already been embedded in the pricing of the goods, so the businessperson could not lose money on the item he/she had bought to sell to people.

The table above already showed how the discount was calculated in the pricing of the good, so whether all of it is given or part of it is given, the actual cost of the good still remains tight.

On the other hand, the table below shows a sample of how the buy-two-get-one-free discount can be calculated.

What this means is that most sellers of physical materials would advertise the "Buy 2 and get 1 free" to pretend to customers that the third item is given freely to them just for buying two items, but what buyers don't know is that the price of the third item has already been divided into two and embedded into the cost of each of the two selling items. See the table below:

Sample of free giving pricing strategy

Unit price for Jif Peanut Butter			Split pack 3 into two for merger	Sell 2 Give 1 Free			New Price
Pack 1	Pack 2	Pack 3		Pack 1	Pack 2	Pack 3	2 for 1 Free
$1.85	$1.85	$1.85	$1.85÷2 = $0$0.925	$2.775	$2.775	$0.00	$5.55

While this strategy not only allows businesspeople to sell more goods for profit, it also denies buyers the economic strategy that says, "Buy wisely to save for tomorrow," and induces citizens to buy unlimitedly. So, even though the buyer doesn't need three packs, he/she is cunningly forced into buying three packs of peanut butter, which makes the businessperson sell more goods at the disadvantage of people's needs.

In economics, we know that *need* is different from *want*, so why buy more peanut butter than you need at a time when you can save the other $1.85 to buy something else that is one of your needs?

In all this, there is enough money collected from the public every day, every month, and every year that is not related to what the businessperson spent from his/her own pocket.

This is how capitalism, or the free market system, beautifully exploits the masses.

Therefore, the amount of money added to goods and collected but not always used up during operational periods explains how company owners amass wealth over the years of the company's existence. This also explains how they give some of the huge piles of money during election years "freely" to the government.

This also means that there is enough money collected by businesspeople that they do not have use for, which brings the entire wealthy world into harmonious agreement with what Solomon the Wise in the Bible described as "Vanity." It is a pity God shares over the world the majority who are suffering poverty when just one man owns more than a tiny country somewhere on earth needs to develop and feed its people.

Now, you may catch a glimpse of why God wants to explain the odds of capitalism, which is a system that created and guaranteed these systems that have created a few citizens as Millionaires and Billionaires in Western countries, where the bulk of each country's population remains poor, working several jobs to earn a living as is called "Pay-Check-To-Pay-

Check" in America. In Liberia, it's called "From-Hand-To-Mouth."

So, please do not get mad at me for the things that are set for discussion on capitalism, which is run by a few at the detriment of the majority.

God revealed to me the hidden truth about the beauty that our world would have had IF mankind had not fallen in love with too much freedom. Let's keep going, and you will understand better.

Electoral College and the people's wills

Oh my gosh, is that democracy for the people?

From the publication of this book, I want the American people to explain exactly how democratic it is for people to stand and sit in the morning, afternoon, and evening, come cold and come sun, to cast their votes in the expression of their wishes then a small group of people gather one evening to vote again to throw away those votes of the majority in deciding who should be the nation's president.

> Can you remember how the male candidate defeated the female candidate in the US elections?
>
> It didn't happen by popular vote but by electoral college vote.
>
> After millions of American people had voted and a female candidate won the popular votes cast by the masses, a fractional group of Americans gathered overnight, threw away the popular votes, and replaced them with the electoral college selection of the male candidate.
>
> This is the guy who "allegedly" sent people later to kill his Vice President and Speaker of the House from certifying the votes of his second term in an attempt to perpetuate himself in power even after he lost to another male candidate in the 2020 elections.

So, the question is, where are the wills of the people who

own democracy? Isn't it suppression of people's wills? Isn't it a subversion of people's choice? Aren't they guilty of covert intents?

I used all these words—suppression, subversion, and covert—on behalf of God to throw back to them the same terminologies they use on others they call "undemocratic societies." Their country cleverly concealed its intent to thwart the wills of its people whenever a particular candidate does not meet the choice of a certain clique who believes it owns the land.

Please tell the world what it means to have a corner vote by a few after ballots have already been cast by the people to whom "democracy" should belong. How different is it when another country holds elections, and then a ruling party corners itself to trash out ballots and replace them with their choice?

The answer from God is that it is cheating, no matter what form it takes. There shouldn't be another vote for the presidency after the general elections. Stop fooling the people into voting when their votes mean nothing.

> Now, we're talking about covert intents, so I want to insert "Court Packing" here for another discussion.
>
> While the US government prepared for general elections in 2020, the current regime focused on appointing more judges to the Supreme Court.
>
> Then I read the news that the sitting president received massive support from the Evangelical Christian group in the US because of his "Pro-life" belief, which led him to appoint conservative or pro-life judges to the Supreme Court.
>
> So, what's the secret behind this? I want us to discuss this from the perspective of covert corruption.
>
> But before anyone challenges the assertion of corruption, let him/her answer the question of intent – What's the intent of court-packing?

Why did God allow him to rule the country?

Firstly, God said it was time to expose the land's imperfection to everyone.

Secondly, God said the president was sent [ahead] to demonstrate the vices I (PAUL) was commanded to count about the land.

Thirdly, the president was also allowed to come ahead to make the world rehearse on the acceptance of rule-breaking [breaking general norms] everyone has followed in the land, just as I (PAUL) was sent not to follow the general practices of how to talk about God or how to write the word of God. For example, instead of me following the old way the Bible has been taught and understood about the black origin, God had mandated me to focus my work on the telling of untold stories that are in the Bible, such as the meaning of the "Fruit of Good and Evil, the Tree of Life, the Garden of Eden, the Ark of Noah, Jesus' forgiveness of the criminal on the cross," and on and on.

> In addition to the three reasons above, I (PAUL) would exercise God's command to discuss several world issues, including the reasons behind terrorism.
>
> The US Capitol attack came on January 6, 2021, upon a sitting body of both the House of Representatives and the House of Senate, organized and perpetrated by US citizens themselves.
>
> So, let us now use them to validate a case study for terrorism in the world. Why do other people resort to violent means branded as terrorism? What is the broad meaning of terrorism if not that the land of many heads masters the acts of terrorism?
>
> Let's go into the book for more details.

As we move closer to them, let's reflect on some terminology revealed earlier, such as greed, ego (self-importance), etc., which are some vices the president exhibited during his tenure.

Oh, How You are falling

Everywhere I went, and whatever I did, except sleep, there was one of the spirits from the theocratic school speaking to my ears about everything happening in democracy and capitalism.

In the forthgoing, I'll try my best to address these issues individually, but for now, let me tell you what God said about the fall of democracy.

Before the spirit [angel] of God told me the message God gave to deliver to me, the story about how God expressed regret over how He designed the Heavens was given to me. He said God designed the Heavens in what the human world now calls autonomy (automatic system).

In God's autonomy system (moving and grabbing freely), He granted the angels self-willpower. In human science today, self-willpower is called a 'chip system.' A chip system is the embedment of specific functionality.

So, God embedded in the angels a functional system that enabled them to move, talk, and do things independently.

However, God had to program them for control purposes. This allows Him to have power over them. This program of control system is what the Bible called 'God's Laws.' That means God gave the angels the freedom to move, talk, and do things by themselves, but they had limits, limits they were not allowed to go beyond. You can call the system of limitation 'restrictions.'

As you might have heard, your pastor preached already about Lucifer's behavior in heaven; he exceeded his limit. He went beyond the restricted point, which means he broke the laws of the Heavens. [Do you see the two ways I spelled 'heaven-Heavens' in this paragraph? The first 'heaven' refers to the place Lucifer tampered with the human souls, while the second 'Heavens' refers to both Headquarters and other spheres {cities} below the Headquarters covered by God's laws].

Because God automated the system [enabled everything functions by itself] and integrated them [linked the angels], He wasn't able to quickly undo [disable] Lucifer as a means of destruction. It required enough time to do so, which is why the Bible says Lucifer (now Satan) would be captured in a short while.

If you analyze every scenario cited above, you may deduce that the system wasn't grown well then, making it impossible for God to disintegrate one of the giant robot machines (angels are God's robots used by Him to do His works in the Heavens). Thus, the time God set to implement the disintegration (fully cut Satan from the system of the Heavens) is what Satan is using to do everything he's doing in the world. He is roaming the earth like a frustrated person out to break everything.

The point is that God regrets why He gave them self-will. Why did He allow them to move or do things freely, which was why Lucifer went against God's laws?

So, the spirit of God said, Satan is the one who sought freedom from God, and he is the architect of freedom who inspired it into mankind. [To understand this, reflect on the scriptures, which say God drove Lucifer and the man out of heaven. Gen. 3:14, 3:23-24. The question to ponder is: Where did the man go when he left God's house? The answer the spirit gave me is that the man went with Satan. So, Satan adopted man and trained him into all his (Satan's) ways- knowledge and trickery].

But why did democracy [this theory of a government system giving people the freedom to choose a leader and do whatever they want] originate from Europe, grow well in Europe, and exported to other countries around the world?

Why didn't every human race practice it but must learn it from Europe {the Western world} the way it is spoken of worldwide?] To get answers to these questions, find my other book, *Interpretation First*, to learn the origin of the government system and white superficial superiority.

That's why most, if not all, of what we know and do, whether science or government system, embody Satan's ways, which is why the world is imperfect, and God must scrap it soon to reinvent it.

Therefore, what mankind calls democracy [with its components of capitalism and human rights] is something God opposes. It violates God's desire for mankind since it takes man away from God's ordinances. God hates it because freedom means getting away from His principles.

Do you see how people in a democracy are violating the Bible every day when their governments enact laws of freedom to do those things the Bible told mankind are not good? Do you see how the nations with democracy are forcing their wills on others by telling them to do what democracy (freedom to do anything) says?

But in my school of the Spirit of God, I was told that democracy would destroy itself soon. It is following the path of Heaven when God's own system was used against Him by His children who rebelled (refused His will). He said democracy will self-destroy.

I have heard these things for almost 16 years now [2024], so when I see Americans [Republicans vs Democrats] arguing and using their own laws to break their own laws for a man who came to power to set the stage for America's global decline through misuse of sanctions and tariffs and wars and disrespect of everyone, even nations, I say democracy is beginning to break itself. When I see new economic, scientific, military, and political alliances around the world, I say democracy [proponent of democracy] is declining. When I see African countries and other neglected countries challenging the hegemonic attitudes of the powers of control, I say democracy is dying. When I see the worship of great powers being attacked, I say democracy is sinking. When I see missiles hitting targets in Israel, I say democracy [the military enforcing it throughout the world], and everything associated with it is crumbling. When I see the US being challenged at the UNGA, I say democracy and everything that fuelled it is dying slowly.

The self-destruct method [party fight] in the leading democratic country in the world is at its worst when you see them using it (democracy) against their own system to prevent punishment on the man who, for the first time in the history of their country, broke his constitutional oath of withholding and defending the law of peaceful transition of power. They have a bunch of evidence against him, but the manipulation and corruption of the system they established and obeyed long ago is preventing them from doing what they know how to do well. It is a sign of weakness within, and everyone who has been lectured on how to do things democratically is watching.

Do you remember how the Egyptian king, Pharaoh, decreed to kill every Hebrew boy child in Egypt? Do you also remember how God used Pharaoh's own daughter to bring into the palace one of the Hebrew children to grow him in the Palace before using him to destroy the Palace? God has His own way of breaking people with their own hands.

So, when God got ready to start breaking down democracy, He allowed the wisest people to choose the very one who would put all things in place to begin the period of decline in the great power. They ignored all the crimes no one had ever been accused of, even to be allowed to run for the presidency. They wouldn't prosecute him even while violating the laws while in office. They wouldn't deny him a presidential run even under state prosecution. They couldn't recognize that the fabric of their system had been attacked within, and this was the beginning of God's work on what the people had done against His word.

How humanity is near to extinction

I have a specific natural infirmity. It eats me to the core. I try to fight it but continue falling like King David would. Still, God chose me, even when I was not a seasoned Christian. That's why I asked Him a question one day in my supplications for a change of my situation.

He gave me two answers: One, he told me the story of Prophet Moses, and He gave me the lesson of Spiritual Induction to teach.

The Prophet Moses' story: When I pleaded for healing of my infirmity, I asked God to take it from me since He wanted to use me, but He said, "Look at Moses." He said the gods of Egypt had struck Moses with stammering to suffer him in the discharge of his [God's] responsibilities. So, when God wanted to send Moses, Moses complained that he could not advocate for the freedom of the Israelites because he lacked better speech. God told me, "I didn't heal Moses of his situation; instead, I gave him Joshua to be his spokesman." He said He doesn't heal every situation in which people are suffering because something called 'Spiritual induction' occurs in the Spirit realm even before people are born into this world. It is a story of how the farmer sowed good seeds, but the wicked one went to plant weeds in the field at night. Thus, everyone has heard what God said about leaving them like that until harvest time.

When I heard this, I fell on my face in shame, knowing I wouldn't get out of my situation. Today, I'm still struggling with it. It has no medical solution, so I'm having a hard time dealing with it, even in my capacity as the messenger.

The Spiritual Induction: The last line of Ezekiel 28:13 (KJV) contains the word 'workmanship.' The reading says the workmanship was prepared in Satan the day he was created.

God interprets the workmanship as trade/skill/knowledge [creative knowledge], which was put in Lucifer, now Satan. It refers to how God trained His children (robot machines) in Heaven to enable them to help Him carry on creation and everything He (God) has to do. This happened before Lucifer rebelled. He went with his skills, which is why the Bible tells us that God didn't take the power from Satan.

Therefore, Satan still participates in every creation, including human creation, since he was initially integrated into the system.

Unfortunately, this is the heavenly science we're talking about here. It is complex to explain for man to understand. It is as difficult to understand as human science would create good things for mankind, but that same thing can be manipulated [used in other ways] to do evil. Imagine the internet system that helps mankind do things faster, but it is the same anyone would use to hack or destroy good things.

So, Satan and his group's role in human creation allows them to manipulate God's good things. This means Satan is the weed planter in God's garden. He is that spirit who puts dirty stuff in everyone before they are born into this world. It explains how some people have high or low sexual desires [human science calls it high or low hormones], some people have anger issues while others have low anger issues [religion says violence and non-violence], some people love material things so much [religion says material greed], some people have the seed of creativity in them, but they need the proper environment and material exposure to grow it [that's how we see people's talents grow faster in the Western world, even now in other technology countries], and the list of things we bear as spiritual seeds in us continue. Satan's involvement in human creation also answers the question of where deformities come from. His involvement explains how people get children from the shrines.

Two, He told me how humanity has violated every law already, but sexual violation is the greatest sin mankind has committed against the Spirit of God as of the time of this book.

The sexual law violation: God passed a law prohibiting promiscuity. He favored marriage and commitment to one woman and one man, but mankind has violated the law worse than anyone can imagine.

The starting argument is how many people can be virgins before marriage and how many remain committed after marriage. The answer is no, not even pastors are qualified.

Unfortunately, not even those who abstain from sex have done good to the Spirit because both the ones who pollute their bodies and those who keep their bodies from sex are starving the Spirit since sex was made to store food in the human body where the Spirit of God would come to feed itself with the energy it needs from the things of the earth. For more details on the importance of sex, go to my books, *Interpretation First* and *Interpretation Fourth*.

The law of murder: Human killing in the human world is the second greatest sin among mankind as of the time of this book.

When the Spirit of God revealed this topic to me in 2006-2008, the reason God led the Israelites to wars in Bible days was unveiled. He compared it to the reason God turned Moses' stick into serpents in Pharaoh's Palace. He said Pharaoh's gods performed magic to turn the magicians' sticks into serpents, which was why God used the same magic to turn Moses' stick into a serpent to destroy Pharaoh's serpents to prove God's superiority to everyone, especially to the Israelites to convince them to put their trust in Him, God.

So, He (God) had to take the Israelites to war to defeat the gods of the lands He promised unto the Jews. But this was for a short while, which was why He put a stop to wars in the story of Jesus telling Peter and the others to put back their swords when he (Jesus) came under attack by the Romans. He didn't only ask them to put back their swords, but he said to them, "No more of this," Luke 22:49-51.

Christians must ask themselves: What happened before Jesus said, 'No more of this?' What was he stopping since he had not been fighting wars such as he came under at that point?

God said the answer is that Jesus was referring to the wars his father had led the Israelites to fight over the years to give them a place they would call home. He said the Jews had now settled down, so they needed to reconcile with their neighbors. That's when he (Jesus) started teaching, 'Love your neighbour as you love yourself, be your brother's keeper,' and other good virtues of the New Testament.

Therefore, God is grieving on His throne right now when He looks down on the earth and sees all the killings going on in His name because He led the Israelites to war in the old, which is interpreted by some people that He approves wars. He said the people inserted their own agenda in the Bible to continue fighting wars instead of being peace ambassadors in the world to settle disputes among nations of non-alliance with God. So, He has some words for the people.

These are the words of God:

[1] You see those killer bombers, those missiles, those chemicals, and everything that you are planning to improve beyond their current capabilities; I (God) have numbered them all as the terror of war on humanity. When they hover over any nation, they are the dragon killer, so the people tremble; they seek hiding places, but you keep chasing them with that eye of an owl bird that shines in the darkness, seeking whom to devour.

[2] You are the cause of the proliferation of weapons in the world as nations struggle hard to achieve deterrence because you wouldn't stop chasing the people in their own countries in your quest to expand your colonization, but you call it "hegemony."

[3] You made enemies for yourselves when you once sat in the middle of the sea and chose to go into the world to turn every culture into yours. You find faults in every person's culture or ways of life, and you perfect yours in the name of God, but use this book as a mirror in which you can see the peck running down your eyes.

[4] You are not defending me (God) because I came to you as Jesus, and I didn't tell Peter to defend Me when the war from Roman authority reached Me. Instead, I told Peter to put back his sword because there was no more fighting. Peace, I preached unto the world and vengeance I left to the judgment time for every man who has been offended. Who are you, seeking to destroy those you call enemies? Are you comfortable being labeled an enemy?

Now you listen, I compromised the word I spoke in the beginning concerning Abel and Cain. I spoke about my hatred for a man killing another, but I was restrained by my desire to prove my superiority to the Israelites, who were doubtful in hearts.

Hear my last word: You're pushing humanity to extinction. You're preparing all the weapons of mass destruction, and others have begun to follow you, too. So, the day is coming when everyone will become tired of living due to disadvantages from you or someone else, and they will choose to use their deadly weapons, not minding if they die too. Humanity will suffer many diseases, and they will die in great numbers, which would mark the beginning of the end time.

God's own attributes He declared Sins

When God examines the people's attitudes in the land, He can't hold back from telling them the truth about what they are doing to the world. So, He revealed to me the things in Him, but Satan took and exacerbated them every day.

The Bible says jealousy/envy, pride/ego, and anger are in the category of wrongdoing (sin), but why would they be wrong when God Himself possesses these attributes?

Jealousy/Envy – I read a sermon delivered by a pastor [anonymous]. In his sermon, he taught that jealousy did not exist until Lucifer [Later known as Satan] became jealous of God. He used, "Your heart was lifted up because of your beauty; You corrupted your wisdom by reason of your splendor. I cast you to the ground; I put you before kings, That they may see you." (Ezekiel 28:17). *He meant that the desire to be exalted/raised high as God got into Lucifer*, and he used, "But you said in your heart, "I will ascend to the heaven; I will raise my throne above the stars of God, and I will sit on the mount of assembly, In the recesses of the north" (Isaiah 14:13), to make his points, but I differ on the assertion that jealousy didn't exist then.

Jealousy existed but was never known until Lucifer exercised it. It existed within God, but He (God) had no competitor until one of His own decided to be like Him.

Jealousy rested inside God like a seed lying dormant in the soil until it was watered to germinate. So, Lucifer's action awakened [watered] jealousy in God.

You can see what time God exercised His jealousy for the first time in the story of Lucifer's action, which caused Adam and Eve to sow fig leaves for themselves, followed by God's action of making them garments as well.

What do I mean? I mean to say that Adam and Eve first did not have an idea of how to cover themselves when God had them naked in the Garden. Still, as soon as Lucifer told them that God was hiding something from them, which is "the knowledge of good and evil," and told them to eat the fruit [the power to enable] that God was still keeping away from them, they obtained the knowledge of making things by themselves. Hence, they sew fig leaves [call them counterfeit clothes] to cover themselves. And because Lucifer had already gone ahead of God to make man gain the knowledge of making garments for themselves, God felt **jealous**, so He made them garments [call this the proper clothes making].

The scenario above is fully explained when you can check the order of the entire episode by reading Genesis 3:1-5,7,21-22.

The second way to know that jealousy existed within

God is that He voiced it to mankind in Exodus 20:5: "*You shall not worship them or serve them*; **for I, the Lord your God, am a jealous God**, visiting the iniquity of the fathers on the children, on the third and fourth generations of those who hate me."

So, God, being the first creation, harbored jealousy in Himself before Lucifer turned against His Will.

Now that God has declared jealousy a sin (the Wrong thing to do), it is time to dig deeper into why or how it became wrong.

Pride/ego – Another thing within God was pride [ego or boastfulness]. Imagine when He speaks boastfully, saying, "I am the Lord your God, who brought you out of the land of Egypt, out of the house of slavery" (Exodus 20:2), and "You shall not profane My holy name, but I will be sanctified among the sons of Israel; I am the Lord who sanctifies you, who brought you out from the land of Egypt, to be your God; I am the LORD", Leviticus 22:32-33.

I assume that a lot of people would argue that it is not a boast, but let me ask how you'd feel if I were speaking of some good that I did for you before and I keep saying, 'I am the one who did it for you, I am the one you must serve alone, because I am the one who did this and that for you.'

God's overuse of I am, I am, is pride that He holds within Himself for doing everything for us, so pride was within Him before Satan started to use it as described in Isaiah 14:13-14: "But you said in your heart, 'I will ascend into heaven; I will raise my throne above the stars of God, and I will sit on the mount of assembly, In the recesses of the north, 'I will ascend above the heights of the clouds; I will make myself the Most High."

So, you see how Lucifer overused 'I' – I will, I will, I will?

Now that He (God) had declared pride as sin or wrong as in Proverbs 8:13: "The fear of the LORD is to hate evil; Pride and arrogance and the evil way and the perverted mouth, I hate," it is time to explain why and how it became a wrong thing to do.

Anger – Another attribute of God that laid within Him until He Himself voiced it out at one point is anger as in Exodus 32:10-11: "Now then let Me alone, that My anger may burn against them and that I may destroy them; and I will make of you a great nation." Then Moses entreated the Lord his God, and said, "O Lord, why does Your anger burn against Your people whom You have brought out from the land of Egypt with great power and with a mighty hand?"

However, He did not outrightly say it is wrong, but rather He cautioned the use of it as in Psalm 37:8: "Cease from anger and forsake wrath; Do not fret-it leads only to evildoing", and in Ephesians 4:31: "Let all bitterness and wrath and anger and clamor and slander be put away from you, along with all malice."

Ending the numeration of these attributes of God with God's caution brings us to the reason why these attributes have been declared evil or why, in fact, He had to caution us.

Satan exacerbates

So, it is evident that jealousy/envy, pride/ego, and anger/temper all existed even before Lucifer rebelled against his creator. And that means he, Lucifer/Satan, did not create them; rather, they are attributes of God, the creator Himself, that were within God, but He never exercised them until Lucifer became a competing force against Him, God.

Now, because Satan began to misuse and overuse them, they became destructive to the plans of God. For example, God revealed to me in 2008 that when He had man naked in the Garden, He had a plan to give man knowledge to do things for himself, but Satan went ahead of Him (God) to reveal to man early the power that enables him to make things.

Remember the conversation that took place between Lucifer and Eve and the result that came out of that conversation.

Lucifer told Eve that God **knew** that if they, *Eve and Adam*, had eaten the fruit that God had told them not to eat, they would not die, but they would be as wise as they (angels and God) were. So, when they ate the fruit, they became wise, and they saw that they were naked, and because they had obtained some enlightenment [call this knowledge] from the fruit, they were able to sew fig leaves [call them clothes] for themselves. The sewing [making things] was the result.

After the encounter between Lucifer and man, see that God came later and gave them garments [call this real clothes or real knowledge of making clothes] as in Genesis 3:21, "The LORD God made garments of skin for Adam and his wife and clothed them, then He addressed the angels as in Genesis 3:22, "Then Lord God said, "Behold, the man has become like one of Us, knowing good and evil; and now, He might stretch out his hand, and take also from the tree of life and eat, and live forever."

The fact that God admitted that Adam and Eve had now become like them (God and the angels) confirmed that there was certain power stored in the "Fruit of knowledge of good and evil." The fact that God came second to give them garments/clothes showed that they were entitled to clothes but did not receive that enlightenment from God first until Lucifer exposed it to them.

According to the enlightenment that I received in 2008, this act of Lucifer was the first to bring out anger from within God. He was stirred up into jealousy, saying that Lucifer [now God named him "Satan," meaning "Turn against or Turn against us or Turn against all our plans] had gone ahead of His plans and was set to do more if He (God) did not act quickly. This led to declaring his capture, but Satan fled from the sphere of the Heavens in which God concentrated His activities at the time, and he (Satan) came down to another sphere of the same milky air to establish his own Kingdom.

Check my first book, 'Interpretation First,' which discusses this fully. In it, I discuss more of the Garden of Eden.

So, Satan is now the one who exacerbates or the master user of these properties of God, which made God declare them sins ["Sin" means "Satan's Intention"].

Now, the overuse of these properties is found among us,

too, human beings, since Satan primarily controls the order of our time.

As we are about to discuss the things that broadly define the people in the land, it was necessary first to give you, their history.

Judgment of the people

In the land, the citizens pride themselves worldwide. They boast or brag about world leadership. They boast of having everything best in the world. They pleasure themselves by criticizing or demeaning others as nothing more than they would love to be treated. They hardly find fault in anything about themselves.

What strikes me most is the enthusiasm most people have when they hear their government plans to destroy other people. They enjoy calling others evil and imposing hardships on others because they're superior.

> A meeting of seven powers:
>
> Seven great powers of the world met and discussed two other powers they considered enemies.
>
> After the meeting, two citizens called on their government to wipe out one of the two so-called enemies.
>
> In a related story, one of the citizens said a friendly member of the seven powers should have wiped out the other people during an old war between the two other people.
>
> The point here is that this attitude of a Christian nation or its citizens desiring [pleasuring in heart] to see other people die and wiped out of the face of this world has been the very reason why peace has left the earth. That's why other nations are getting interested every day in possessing weapons of mass destruction to counter these threats of annihilation.

Because this spirit of ***pride*** fills their hearts, the spirit of ***jealousy/envy*** finds better space in their hearts. When they see other people growing in knowledge, the spirit of ***fear*** comes down on them and thrusts them into ***anger*** and dissatisfaction, which thrusts them further into preparations for war.

They continue to make new or more weapons, moving them everywhere they perceive threats and strangulating others with harsh conditions. They move around everywhere to turn brothers and sisters against one another.

They are cunning. They use gifts to impress and buy people's interests to go against their neighbours, but their interest is to break their friends and foes down to become kings above all. When everyone in the land fights among themselves and breaks down their houses, they [sitting deep in the sea] would come up like a rescuer to plunder the people's resources. In everything they do with a friend, their interest is the ultimate priority.

Greed overwhelms them. Greed is the excessive desire for anything.

Greed is not a spirit of God. God created everything and owned it all. He is the wealthiest creature ever. So, He has no room in His heart for greed.

Therefore, greed is a small spirit that originates from Satan's kingdom. He uses greed for enforcement to get more of what he wants. That's why greedy people never find rest in everything they do. They keep on wanting and wanting and wanting because an enforcer is forcing them to want more to give to him.

So, the image of the sea with many heads uses its many

heads to grab from here to there. It wants everything in the land, so it pours out fire, cold, smoke, darkness, and suffering to achieve everything and anything it desires. That's why there is so much trouble in the lands.

Let's see how greed affects citizens in capitalism.

> Greed for money has created "The Game of Money" in the world, where everyone participates. So, countries' citizens hardly notice the harm this game causes.
>
> To demonstrate that, I have one scenario that deals with the buy-and-sell practice in the housing business.
>
> In the housing game, a house is bought at, say, $300,000.00, and then sold at a higher price later, say, $380K to $400K. This cycle continues, with the subsequent sale of the same house expected to reach $450/500K in the next few years, perpetuating the escalating nature of the housing market.
>
> As you can see from the above transactions, based on what prices look like in 2020, a house that goes for $300K this year may have started at $100K or less some years ago.
>
> This trend tells us that house prices are not expected to decrease in the future but to continue climbing. This steady increase in housing prices could have significant long-term consequences for housing affordability in the country.
>
> While this demonstrates the high cost of living in high-income societies, it is concerning that citizens do not see anything wrong with it. The fact that this 'game' remains a lucrative business for banks and the housing industry, with no significant public outcry or pressure on the government to address the issue, underscores the need for collective action.
>
> Hence, economists are not working towards decreasing living costs; instead, they are increasing costs to make more money.

Greed is a powerful spirit of destruction. It breaks peace and unity and is the cause of many current wars.

Starting with why the most powerful country elected a president who wasn't qualified but was chosen because of his wealth, greed played a significant role in the elections.

The candidate himself was greedy. During the campaign, many stories emerged about his business history. He had a history of cheating contractors, inflating costs, evading taxes, and more. Still, the people selected him. If you ask me, I will say it was because many business communities that support elections believed he would use his tricks to bring wealth to them personally.

To prove me right, consider what his administration did to other countries' businesses. He imposed sanctions on other major countries and companies. These sanctions aimed to give his country's enterprises leverage over other countries' businesses.

Unfortunately, a new administration saw nothing wrong with his policies, so it continued from where he stopped. The end result triggered a divided world, with countries lining up for a new way of doing business. These are aimed at each country's own interest in making more money. Greed is the propellant.

Even the wars going on at the time of this book are based on greed for control of land, to grab its natural resources, and to enrich oneself.

But his noise about "Let's make everything in our country to sell to the world" is bad for other countries because it has the highest propensity to encourage the entire world to buy goods at high prices. Disrupting competition to monopolize everything would infuse high pricing.

This leads me to ask these three questions: Why can't high-income countries produce high-quality goods for themselves and allow low-income countries to produce low-quality goods for themselves to develop their economies slowly before buying high-quality goods? Isn't that how high-income countries started before they reached the peak of producing high-quality products? We have a big world, so why must high-income countries produce everything to force every poor individual and community to buy at high prices?

As I said, I stand to be corrected, so I am writing this piece that is solely my opinion about some goods that I have bought in the US, which I found faulty, to my greatest surprise, regarding durability. For example, in November 2021, my wife and I junked out the couches we bought from "The American Furniture Store" here on Auburn Blvd, Sacramento, in December 2015. Although they started peeling in just one year, we took so long to junk them only because we didn't want to buy new couches until we were ready to move to a new house. The peeling was so bad that we had to order a couch cover online from Amazon to cover the long couch we used most. And just two months after purchase, one of the handles of the upper drawer of a dresser screwed out and couldn't be put back. The body of the same dresser is not water resistant, so the black coating wears out whenever water drops on it.

Although not everything that we bought from American Furniture has problems, we're keeping an old couch in our garage that was bought before the American Furniture types, not necessarily because it is bad but because it is too old, as it was more than two years old, from a different store before buying the ones from American Furniture. This emphasizes how some things are durable while others are not in America.

Some people may argue that nondurable things are not American but imported. Still, I'll differ somehow because almost all overseas companies are American joint ventures, so whatever is made in that country has some American input. On the other hand, the American government's customs allow [should allow] goods into America based on the assessment that those goods meet their quality test. Therefore, if they allow goods from other countries that are not of good quality per the American standard, then who is to blame if everything in America must be like Americans' own?

So, if there are shoddy goods in the US, why would anyone think that everything made in America will be of high quality despite the high price tag, especially since America is one of the highest-income countries in the world?

So, this make-in-our-country syndrome is one primary reason why the president was chosen for the second term to "stand up to their perceived rival country." Because he puts himself above others so much, I see him as one of the most envious persons in his country who hates to see others progress above him, which is why envy is discussed in this book as one of the vices destroying world peace and unity.

The president is also full of anger, and I think they believed they could exploit it from him to bring down countries that are opposed to things they want them to do – bow down to their lifestyles, as exemplified in this book, allow their companies set up businesses in other countries to bring more wealth back home, use their money alone to boost their economy to enable them to enforce their power everywhere.

What are the aftereffects for the US?

When I first published this book in 2021, the world was not what it is by 2024, so I want to [personally] look at what's happening to the US.

This is not coming from a vacuum; rather, it is from the things that the Spirit of God enlightened me on about government systems, science and technology, the money system, the causes of war, and more.

[1] The US had long been employing several economic strategies aimed at benefiting them even at the detriment of others. One such strategy is building manufacturing outside their homeland to other countries, such as China, because they would pay lower wages and little or no taxes to those governments. As a result of paying low wages and little or no taxes to other countries for using their lands and human

resources to manufacture their products, they sell them at high prices and make more profits.

It was easy for them in other countries, but China struck a deal with the US businesses when they went to China. The business community reported this arrangement of knowledge sharing to the US government and was accepted because the government wanted to make more money out of China. Well, everybody was happy. The US business is making more money while China is learning from them how to develop technology. It was a win-win situation. No one forced anyone.

However, several years after learning from the US and European companies, Chinese people began to build their own technology companies. This must prove to you that the Chinese people, like every other human, bear the seed of science [knowledge] in them, but the seed of knowledge in every man remains dormant [sleeping] until it receives proper nourishment. The nourishment of knowledge is the creation of the appropriate condition necessary for the growth of the seed of knowledge planted in every man before birth.

The seed of knowledge (creativity) varies from one person to another. It also differs from one human color (race) to another. [Check my other book, Interpretation First, for more information on the seed of knowledge, written in the Bible as the tree of good and evil]. That's why the Chinese picked up the speed of developing technology as soon as they got the proper exposure to those who took years and effort to build it.

The Chinese are the wisest people in this game of the Americans using other people to develop themselves. The

Chinese government traded their human resources for what they needed, and the Western governments traded their knowledge for the wealth they needed.

So, when I hear American politicians tell their citizens that China took their manufacturing jobs, I get upset because it wasn't China that came to America for American companies; instead, it was the same American political group who told their business community to go into China to build factories to pay little in wages to the Chinese people to produce goods that they, the Americans, would bring back to their country and take out to the entire world for profit making.

[2] When American political group often lecture their citizens that China's rules forced American companies to give US technology ideas before they could do business in China, I laughed at the telling to be childish because they were not ignorant of business deal-making and that China made such rule a bargaining chip in allowing Americans to do businesses on Chinese soil while paying their Chinese citizens little dollars in wages. In that instance, it was left to the Americans to have rejected the deals as creepy infringement, but instead, they accepted the deals because they knew that they were going to benefit from the Chinese while the Chinese also accepted whatever conditions the Americans gave since they, the Chinese, knew that they too were going to have the opportunity to learn from the American's presence.

Here, I greatly admire the Chinese investment strategy that Africans did not apply to Europeans and Americans when Westerners went to Africa to invest in bringing goods back to European and American cities. Africans did not adopt this strategy, which is why they have been underdeveloped up to now despite the centuries-old business relationship between them and the Western world.

Western powers dictated every business term to Africans, so African countries were not able to adopt the modern scientific methodology of manufacturing and create more jobs for their citizens.

Reflecting, I see that what the Chinese did was a reverse approach to the Japanese style of the Meiji Restoration of 1868-1912; of interest to me is that "The Meiji sent young men to study abroad and learn new traits from the West." So, in reverse, the West (Americans) went to the Chinese, and the Chinese seized the opportunity to learn from the West by giving them the condition to share their ideas with the Chinese. What is the evil in this bargaining agreement? Can we call it a fair deal of Pro quo Pro – We let you use our land and human resources to make your goods for little pay, and you teach us how you do your things?

[3] When politicians tell their citizens that the Chinese are in the habit of stealing technology from Americans, I also laugh at the selfish way of thinking of others when there is evidence of America taking Soybeans from the Chinese and developing them into an export good to many countries, including China, where they originated.

Since we live in a world of internet systems, why can't you search "History of Soybean?"

So, why are Americans crying about being cheated on by the Chinese, taking technology ideas too from the Americans that the Chinese have now developed into an advanced level of 5G internet connectivity? Are we not seeing too much **envy** here for the Chinese to advance the development of internet technology that they took from the Americans? Are we not seeing too much **jealousy** here that speaks to why Americans cannot continue to lead in this field? Are we not seeing too much selfishness [**pride**] here on the part of Americans for not accepting to work with others to gain from them, even when the other people prove innovative at things that the people have taken from the Americans just like Americans have done too in the soybean and other areas from the Chinese and other countries that now brings wealth to American farmers and industries?

More on self-centeredness, let's look at the space exploration issue. The US opposed China's desire to join the International Space Station (ISS) in 2011: Why China Was Banned from the International Space Station | Space (labroots.com), but today China has made tremendous achievements all by itself, making history as first country in Space to land on the far/dark side of the Moon: China Makes Historic Landing on 'Dark Side' of the Moon - HISTORY as recently as January 3, 2019 as opposed to the more than 50 years of America's presence in Space. China has now developed its own satellite system, "Beidou Navigation Satellite System (BDS)," to enable the country to take pictures of the earth and its cities and monitor them just as the US and its allies with the GPS.

Now we're talking about space exploration; please allow

me to give you another piece of news from space: news from the people we cannot see with our naked eyes.

In 2006, I was told in my school of the Spirit that what human science now reports as space exploration, which is man's attempt to leave the earth to live in outer space above the physical earth, is what the Spirit reported or predicted in parable to us in the Bible as man's construction of a building from the earth to the heavens.

Now, the Bible tells a story about the Tower of Babel, so let's get something straight about it first by analyzing Genesis chapter 10, which comes before chapter 11.

In chapter 10, the Bible says Noah's three sons have already born children who built different cities and spoke different languages, including Ham's descendants, who made up ancient Egypt, Canaan, and Cush, all with their own languages. Notably, chapter 10:4 gave an account of Javan's sons – Elishah, Tarshish & Kittites "from whom the Maritime peoples spread out into their own territories by their clans within their ***nations***, each with its own ***language***."

The question for our analysis is, how, in chapter 11, can anyone say that the people spoke one language until their building collapsed in chapter 11 before different languages came on to earth, after chapter 10 says there were nations and languages already? Isn't that something was misunderstood from what Moses called the "Tower of Babel?"

We must understand that as soon as Noah came down from the boat, his children started to populate the Middle East today, where the biblical tribes are found. The same Bible says they began to speak in different languages, which means that they were not living together to build a tower as it has been perceived by those early interpreters of Moses's work, so it is impossible for the whole world to have spoken one language until a so-called tower collapsed.

However, as one of my manuscripts, "*Interpretation First*," currently undergoing publication review, will tell us, the word "Bible" means "Two Worlds," which means God's word was written about two different Worlds with identical events. The two Worlds are the *Spiritual World,* where God and His invisible and soft-body children live, and the *physical world,* where we, the hard-body children of the same God, live.

The picture of these two Worlds is simple to grasp from the Book of Revelation when John clearly distinguished another Jerusalem that he saw in the Spirit realm from the Jerusalem he knew on earth that anyone can take a plane to go to see in Israel today. Even in the Book of Genesis, we have the privilege to read about water, trees, rocks, minerals, streets, and other names or things that are Spiritual, just as we have them on earth here with us.

That's why the Interpretation First book contains a structural (step-by-step) explanation of the evolution of man and Noah's two worlds' existences. In the first world, Noah became one of the last day generations of that spiritual world in which spiritual science was at its highest peak in those last days of their living. Noah could build a "Boat," but in an actual sense, it means a large ship that carried large cargo like elephants and anything you can think about.

Let me ask you this second question: In that first world before it was destroyed, if Noah was actually a physical man and had built a "Boat," which the Spirit told me was a ship like an aircraft carrier today, why didn't ancient men start our world with the building of large vessels capable of carrying elephants and any heavy weights? Instead, they [first humans] didn't have the slightest idea of building anything at all, so they [historically] lived in caves and hollows of woods until after several other generations before the construction of canoes and other smaller floating carriers came about, even before such water vessels, such as boats and ships capable of carrying elephants and other large animals were recently built.

So, the story that the people were constructing a building to reach the heavens is a big parable told in the Bible to tell us that in the last days of physical man's existence, there will also be advanced science, just as it was in the last days of the First World. This means that in the last days [end time], physical humans would want to go live in the heavens, otherwise called "Outer Space" in human science.

To better understand that Noah's first world existence was Spiritual, you can start analyzing man's history in the two worlds: In the beginning, the Bible says that man was naked in the Garden [Woods], and at the beginning of our physical world, human history tells the same story that early man didn't wear clothes unlike we do today; instead, they were naked in the jungles [Woods] as they roamed those bushes. The Bible says man sewed leaves and wore them as clothes, then our early man's history holds it that our ancient fathers tied leaves around themselves to cover the genital parts; the Bible says later man received clothes from God, then our human history tells us that another generation of early men received the knowledge of weaving even before we modern men started to use sophisticated machinery today for clothes making.

Using the same Bible story of man's nakedness in the garden, one can also imagine that man wasn't living in any house, which is the same as our forefathers didn't live in houses at first but lived in hallows of woods and holes in the hills and sometimes out in the open colds until another generation of mankind began to build thatched huts then mud huts then brick houses and now concrete houses in our time of this book.

But the Bible is silent on many other things, such as when Noah came out of the boat as the first human being like him, who and his children didn't have a fire but ate raw food. Then, the fire was discovered later, after several centuries, by a different generation. In fact, historically, early men didn't have implements at first, so they strangled animals with their bare hands to eat until several centuries before another generation began to make implements like machetes, axes, and so on.

These are just a few examples of how the Spirit of God told me to explain to the world that the first world was a Spiritual existence of things that have been replicated in the physical world. This is the same reason why everything that was told in the Bible about the first world repeats until it reaches its end.

Therefore, no matter how far human science goes with its space exploration to live there, there shall come a day and time when they shall be brought down to rubble, with no escape from what God had promised He would do.

[4] When I see countries shunning Huawei 5G, reasoning with the US that the Chinese will spy on them or fearing to lose business with the US nation if they do business with Huawei, I get even more upset over the idea that countries are not willing at all to tell the American people that the level of monopoly they have been exercising over everything in the world must be reduced.

The worst is that Asian nations are not sensitive enough to the danger America's presence in their countries poses to the peaceful existence of their regions. They are blaming China for expanding claims over water and other pieces of land that they, the different countries, which are sharing borders with China without checking their own actions of letting the Americans use those nearby areas to plant weapons of mass destruction for China. I mean that they are enabling America to build nuclear arsenals in their countries while ignoring the fact that this is America's strategic way of continuously using other lands to fight her wars, destroying those lands with chemical weapons, and forcing those same countries to come bowing and begging the US for economic assistance to help them rebuild their war-torn countries. This is the US strategy of break-them-to-rebuild-them.

Let me ask this question: how would the US feel if they saw China come one morning to plant a missile right in Mexico to the very proximity of the US? Umm, if it's not good for you, then why should it be good for another? Why should China be comfortable with US military alliances with all her surrounding neighbors, where all heavy weaponry is stationed and ready at any time to be used against China in any event of war?

It's just this year, 2024, when I heard the first news of a Chinese spy plane with a Russian plane coming near the US coast—it's not a warship. As expected, the US got furious to see that happen. They sent their F-16s right away. That's how terrific it can be when the Chinese see US planes, ships, and missiles near the Chinese coast or in its backyard country.

Take the Chinese shoe and wear it to see how it feels on them. So, why would the US continue to patrol the seacoast of China, not just with commercial vessels but also with Aircraft carriers, in the name of sailing an international route?

[5] When I heard that the US was criticizing China's Belt and Road initiative by telling other countries that it was a debt trap, I got even more upset over the acceptance of such rhetoric by these Belt and Road participating countries. Thankfully, the situation is getting clearer and more apparent, so now there are opposing views to the narrative.

Firstly, China's intention to help other countries get infrastructurally developed is brilliant and emancipating from the Western method of focusing on building their Western infrastructures alone with money drawn from the businesses they do with under-developed countries worldwide.

For several decades of doing business with African countries, the US and European nations have not focused on ways to make African countries build massive infrastructures, or at least their approach to how it should have been done was not effective.

So, if China came up with a new idea to build every

country to look well-developed like China or Western countries, what is wrong with that? If participating countries are not able to negotiate better terms with China or are not able to pay their debts back to China, just as they also owe several million dollars in debts to Western lending clubs such as the IMF and World Bank, then why would China be the devil here?

So, let's see how Pakistan has sought almost 20 bailouts from the IMF for half a century by clicking the link below in the Yahoo Finance 2022 news report, which says, "Pakistan Seeks to End 50 Years of IMF Debt with ESG Bond." Then, we can tell ourselves whether Western countries have not debt-trapped their borrowers; only China is now the newest lender in the world.

https://finance.yahoo.com/news/pakistan-seeks-end-50-years-210000467.html

I'm so upset with countries that buy this rhetoric from the Americans or the West when they cannot see that Americans, or the West want to continue to hijack the people who have been overlooked and marginalized over the centuries in terms of how God wants the whole world to look.

This means God wishes to see the whole world be infrastructurally, technologically developed, and beautiful.

Well, I think I'm not upset anymore because the pendulum is swinging towards a new era of multipolarity. This means these "under-developed" countries are now willing to ignore whatever the West holds against Socialism/Communism by focusing on whatever good thing emanates from Communist China regarding the new

Internet of things, low prices for goods, and infrastructural development.

They are doing this by sitting with China to revisit the deal-making process to better carry on the BRI vision.

The question is: Where were these ideas before, or why didn't they do this all these years?

But just this month, December 2021, I read a news article that might explain why they neglected Africa's infrastructural development. The news I came across on my phone on December 2, 2021, shocked me because there is now a discussion on the effect infrastructural development may have on Africa's ecosystem. The mere fact that some people are now concerned about road effect on the ecosystem when it comes to Africa's development issues brings me the question: is this the reason why Western nations developed their countries by destroying their ecosystems but turned blind eyes to Africa's infrastructural development over the years, not until China introduced her BRI initiative? For more information on this, click the link: https://phys.org/news/2021-12-africa-road-network-affect-ecosystems.amp.

Imagine that America has just entered into a pact with Taiwan to replicate China's Belt and Road model in the Asian Pacific region, planning to raise Millions of dollars to help carry on the same infrastructural development projects in that region. See this link: US, Taiwan alternative to China's BRI - JournalsOfIndia.

Just as I submitted the manuscript of the first edition of this book to my publishing company for review in December 2021, I was reading another news story on my phone as I do every early morning, this time about the European Union, too, readying its own African infrastructural development package to "counter China's Belt and Road strategy." For more information, click the link: EU Belt And Road Initiative For Africa—Bing News.

What the Western powers, the US and EU, readiness to offer China's module of infrastructural development in the Asian Pacific region and Africa at this late moment shows me is how good ideas originate from Communism or Communist China, too. These ideas are worth emulating to help the world become a better place for all, as compared to what the Democratic world has taught or refused to do over the centuries. So, why the hate and propaganda against China?

Thankfully, developing countries are waking up to the reality that they need science and technology. This would fulfill the message I received from the Spirit World about Africa's development time. I heard the message clearly in 2008 that Africa is about to receive science and technology to build its infrastructure and create jobs for its citizens. I was told that Africa is about to become a full member of the comity of nations to have a voice on the international stage, not a mere listener anymore.

So, Africans are not shunning China anymore. They are not distracted by the rhetoric of the West anymore when the West is not respecting the so-called "international norms" they alone set up in the past to govern everything, such as (a)the laws governing waters that were meant to grant Western sailors rights to travel to the shores of any country around the world since they were the first to start traveling far away into other people's lands around the world, (b)the laws governing business transactions since they were the first to come to trade with different races, [c]the laws governing the uses of money [monetary systems] since they were first to use money widely as the medium of exchange, and [d]the laws governing what is called human rights now that they use everywhere to introduce their cultural ways of life to all people, and on and on?

Maybe this is the eye-opening moment when everyone can see how they are now changing these rules or laws to benefit themselves while they continue to hold others accountable under the laws. At the same time, they don't want to be held accountable under these same laws when they violate them, such as America's refusal to answer charges of war crimes and other crimes against other people around the world, including the current situation involving the Russia-Ukraine and Israel-Palestine wars. In these two wars, the West continued to supply weapons to Ukraine and Israel, influencing the two countries not to end the wars and the killing and suffering of people.

It is clear now that the purpose of creating the United Nations is not respected anymore because those who established it are the same people declaring wars on other countries every day. The US and its Western allies have invaded many countries, Iraq being the perfect example. This always happens when they feel that a small country is not obeying their Western practices. Still, when another big country goes against a small nation for not obeying them, the West would accuse that non-Western country of violating international laws or abusing the sovereign rights of another, as in the case of Russia to Ukraine.

I have heard the argument that Russia's invasion is aimed

at annexing Ukraine, so it is against the UN's charter. Still, the US has been invading other countries through different means, including military and sanctions, to establish their influence over the people. This different strategic warfare has caused almost the entire world to get the US and its European ally's consent on decisions small nations take concerning these countries' internal issues.

That's why I ask: Is this not the annexation of nations to the US's list of land and influence when the US compels other nations through their strategic warfare to station its troops, ways of life, and businesses in those countries just as it would freely do in its homeland across the Atlantic?

The Covid-19 Conflict

The issue of COVID-19 explains stereotyping and conflicts in our world. The stereotyping in this topic represents the gap created by human pride.

Wuhan

The disease that the World Health Organization labeled "COVID-19" in January 2020 must be why people and nations must be cautious about what they say about other people or nations.

It was a new sickness, but its symptoms were similar to those of the flu virus. It was previously reported to have first been detected in a local market area in Wuhan, China.

While everyone around the world was blaming China, my thoughts were different in the sense that the Chinese people may have first thought it was the usual flu virus and that it could have been cured. Hence, they began to fight it while keeping any public announcement secret. Keeping the information secret may have been a mistake by Xi's government. Still, it is not a new practice by any government to have medical secrets that focus on studying a particular disease that may have originated in a particular region.

Well, they later found out that it was a strange and new kind of sickness, so they sent the information to the China office of the World Health Organization (WHO) on December 31, 2019.

The US, which has already been against China on trade issues, ceased on the time it took China to report to the world about the new disease, accusing China of deliberately hiding information regarding the latest virus that has begun to infect people all over the world.

Surprisingly enough, China's neighbor, Australia, quickly announced that it had joined the US in condemning China for keeping the virus secret from the world. While China was still struggling with massive death tolls, Australia then blew a trumpet call to China to let the World Health Organization enter that country immediately to ascertain facts about the origin of the virus.

This call was not wrong, but it had the wrong timing. It ran counter to the practice that when a man's house is on fire, you first help to rescue the man's family and let his nerves cool down before asking him questions in detail about the cause of the fire. When we let a person cool his nerves first, it is believed that the person would be in his right senses to recollect facts about the circumstance.

For the US, the Trump administration didn't waste any time labeling the virus as the "China Virus," thereby exploring proposals to punish China or demand financial compensation.

As the virus spread to every corner of the world, infecting roughly 1,500,000 people in March 2020, Western scientists began to attribute the outbreak to the eating of what they called "Chinese Bats and Pangolins." They proposed a ban on eating those creatures in China and worldwide. They said the virus originated from bats and pangolins, which are good delicacies in China. This theory followed the same path that the West said about the origin of HIV, AIDS, and the Ebola viruses. See the following reports from Google search.

1. **How did the first person catch AIDS?**

Scientists believe the first human who got HIV was a person in Africa. This happened when Simian Immunodeficiency Virus (SIV) went from apes or chimpanzees to humans. This virus probably crossed humans by **contact with monkey blood** while cutting up monkeys to eat.

2. **Origin of the Ebola virus:**

The Ebola virus, causing outbreaks of fatal infection, is transmitted from infected animals such as fruit bats, chimpanzees, and monkeys to humans via their blood, secretions, and meat.

As an African writing this book, I can tell you how I hunted monkeys in Liberian forests and used swinging clothes to trap down bats at night, which I ate while in my teens. Now that I have been testing negative for HIV every year since 2015, when I started doing HIV tests in the US, I now write this book to challenge Western scientists to prove why all Africans who have eaten monkeys are not sick with Ebola and AIDS viruses, except when they get infected through the known means of sexual intercourse and other transmission processes. I also want them to go into African and Chinese forests, then grab several thousand species of these animals to check them to prove that all monkeys and bats in Africa and China are infected with AIDS, Ebola, and COVID-19 viruses IF at all the infecting of some animals with viruses has not been the result of western scientists' works of using animals to test new chemicals/drugs around the world.

My point remains that Western countries have taken pleasure in demeaning and calling other races evils. They find joy in ascribing the origin of diseases to other races, including condemning other races' foods, cultures, and traditions over the centuries.

Where did COVID-19 come from- Wuhan or Italy?

This same Western attitude of dumping the ugly on other races has just happened between Wuhan and Italy.

Despite scientific evidence showing that the disease now known as COVID-19 existed in Italy [Europe] in different variants and earlier than in Wuhan [China], the West still says that the disease originated in China before coming to Italy.

While the World Health Organization (WHO) is searching for the origin of COVID-19, they're looking nowhere like Italy. Every effort is directed towards China alone to prove the theory that the virus originated from China and only China. How partial is that!!!

Besides the known fact that China and the US, or the fact that all technology countries hold secrets to themselves for what they do and how they do them, the US/West demanded China to turn over their laboratory secret documents to them, which is not only an attempt to get Chinese's scientific secrets but to also make China vulnerable to the US's/West's intrusions into grabbing everything that the Chinese have been doing in their country. Can Americans, Germans, French, or British do this with their most advanced medical facilities?

But China also has advanced medical experts who didn't sit dumbly waiting for Western scientists to tell them lies about the disease. Chinese epidemiologists worked hard to identify the different COVID-19 variants around the world to overturn that Western narrative.

Other reports outside China say the novel coronavirus running rampant around the world is not the Wuhan variant but a variant that mutated in north Italy, as German news agency Weser Courier reported, citing a virologist, Prof. Alexander Kekule.

I took some excerpts from the CGTN News report in 2020 just as below:

Captioned as - **99% of Covid-19 cases traced back to north Italy: Top German virologist**.

The report said and I quote, "The novel coronavirus running rampant around the world is not the Wuhan variant, but a variant that mutated in north Italy, top German virologist Alexander Kekule said on Thursday."

The report also said the Italian strain is called G Variant, which has genetic mutations. It is likely to be more contagious than the one found in Wuhan, which was the epicenter of the Covid-19 outbreak that first occurred in China.

In fact, the German news agency Weser Courier cited the virologist saying, "Over 99% of the Covid-19 cases can be genetically traced back to the Italian variant, and even the current cases in China are reimported from Europe and the rest of the world."

For more information, click this link: what did alexander kekule says about covid-19 in italy - Bing

The New Tool of Human Control

The Bible is the **first tool** of control used by Westerners to conquer the rest of the world. It was used to teach submission and endurance with little or no resistance. It weakened the minds of Africans so much that they abandoned their scientific practices. They deemed them generally evil, just as the healing herbs were not advanced because they were taught to be evil powers. Still, the Westerners kept advancing theirs. Check my other book, Interpretation First, for details.

The **second tool** of control they used was science and technology. Science is the creative arts every human was born with. The Africans had it like all others, but again, they abandoned advancing it. Check my other book, Interpretation First, for details. The Westerners advanced theirs and used their factories to conquer and control the world.

The actual existence of God was a strong theory taught long before science emerged powerful, and then science began to challenge that theory. Science started to create materials in physical terms and laid down formulas that anyone can follow to do the same thing others have done before, so modern men took much belief in science over God, gradually displacing the strong sense that God exists and is powerful.

The **third tool** of control is human rights. This tool is used with a government system called democracy and a money system called capitalism—the right to vote, the right to get whatever you want, etc.

So, human rights is a new teaching that has emerged recently. This teaching has dominated daily activities in the world, putting the greatest threat to the things that were taught about God's Laws.

In all my books, I have explained God's hatred towards so many human practices under the brand name of human rights for today's generation, among which is the practice of wrong sexual routes. Still, in this book, we will talk about a new lifestyle called 'Nakedness or nudity' that is most recently gaining prominence.

Nowadays, it is a pleasure to make what is meant for the bedroom between two loved ones a public display under human rights permission.

Women are fully aware of what to do to tickle their loved ones, and like I said in my other book, *Interpretation First*, the women's spirits came down from Heaven lately to redeem the women of the world from abuse and downtrodden. Still, the weapon they came with is their body, which is what their Queen and her early assistants used in the Spirit Realm to penetrate Satan's kingdom before pouring out into the physical world to introduce women's freedom, which is now called the "Women's Rights" movement today. In all of it, men are their captives and slaves now, thereby turning the table against men who initially enslaved women at the beginning of our world system. So, gradually, they're taking over the world through the power of their bodies, and that is what the world is experiencing now through the celebration of women's festivities, which can be seen on stages when women models appear on stage in different genital displays as is in several pictures from this link: Women Wearing Slips, Bras, Panties, Hose and Pantyhose (thehypertexts.com) as is being embraced by western cultures.

Since the Western world now controls everything around the world, human rights teaching has uplifted and heavily aided other cultures, as in this link Caribbean girls dance - Bing.

This topic is important because Western countries, especially the United States, claim and boast of being the good people whom God has favored most. They print the Bible in large volumes, display it in their homes, and recite it as a Western ritual to demonstrate that they are the people of God. But they are very fond of misusing the very book, gradually replacing the Bible with the laws of their choice, such as Human Rights Laws that are now enshrined in their constitutions of the dos and don'ts.

Since they have demonstrated commitment to God before the entire world, God has chosen them from the peoples of the human world to point out everything He shall judge in Heaven. He is on His last tour of the earth to announce the coming of His wrath, even while everyone seems to be in love with science and Human Rights to do anything they like while forgetting the laws and the things He wrote about the First World. That's why this book can otherwise be called the pre-judgment book. It is only meant to point out the things we are doing wrongly on earth. Still, it is not a Bible to teach righteousness; instead, it is a supportive book to the Bible for simplifying our activities on earth.

So, let us go into the Bible before addressing our topic today about nakedness.

In the Bible that you got in your homes, it is written: [9] Then the Lord God called to the man and said to him, "Where are you?" [10] He said, "I heard the sound of You in the garden, and I was afraid because I was naked; so I hid myself," Genesis 3:9-10.

When God saw that they had already received the knowledge of things, He had no other choice but to do what was necessary, so the Bible says, "The Lord God made garments of skin for Adam and his wife and clothed them" (Genesis 3:21).

The action of God giving them clothes was followed by God admitting certain truths and giving a caution to the angels, as in Genesis verse 3:22. (1) God admitted that man became one of them, which reads, "Then the Lord God said, 'Behold, the man has become like one of us, knowing good and evil." (2) Then God cautioned the angels to not allow man take from the tree to eat and live forever. This is written as, "And now, he might stretch out his hand, and also take from the tree of life, and eat, and live forever."

But before we continue, let me make a point clear:

Starting from Genesis 3:4 to end at 3:22, you will understand that Lucifer told Eve that God knew that if they (Eve and her husband) had eaten the fruit, they were not going to die but their eyes were going to open, and they would be like God, knowing good and evil.

You will also notice that after eating the fruit, their "eyes were opened" so that they saw themselves naked, and they sew fig leaves (counterfeit clothes) for themselves to cover their nakedness.

This act of them eating the fruit had been interpreted to me by the Spirit of God in 2008 as the receiving of science, or the receiving of the power/knowledge that enables to self-create.

The Spirit then said to me that while Satan is not to be glorified for being the first to giving this knowledge of creation to man, it is nevertheless time to reveal the truth about what really transpired in Heavens at the beginning of all things concerning mankind. So, the Spirit of God said to me again that this attitude of Lucifer is what constituted his disobedience towards God and disregard to all the heavenly Laws that governed the timing of things.

To best understand the truth that scientific knowledge was due man, in Genesis 3:21 God then fulfilled man by giving him/them (Adam and Eve) clothes and He called them "Garments", which had been interpreted to mean real science or real knowledge to make things for themselves, and this became the mortarboard on which every science that comes to man lays, even if it comes from Satan today.

Furtherance to that, in Genesis 3:22, God admitted to the angels that "the man has now become like one of us, knowing good and evil".

Up to date, man has been exercising this **good** (building/constructing) and **evil** (breaking down/destroying).

Now, let's discuss these three points:

1. The man (Adam and Eve) said they were **naked (nude)** and were afraid (ashamed) of God.

What the Bible tells us here but has never been understood by theologians is that the man and his wife dwelt together in pure nakedness when they were yet ignorant of the knowledge of creating things. They dwelt together in half-naked clothes (covering only their front parts with leaves) but became shameful upon the approach of someone, but God came by.

2. Due to the shame of nakedness or half-nakedness, they **hid themselves**.

This section implies that before God came by, they knew that their nakedness was not to be seen by anyone, even not God, so they hid themselves behind the trees.

3. God realized that it was no longer good for man to remain naked, so He made **garments** for them.

This authenticates the fact that God Himself didn't purpose man to be naked, so when He saw that Lucifer had already opened their eyes and they could see everyone wearing clothes, He provided them with strong clothes from the skin, supposedly the skin of an animal, and this was the implanting of real science.

This knowledge that was passed on to man, in the beginning, was poured out into the physical as a human science, and it has been developing from ancient men wearing leaves. They wore animal skins, then they began to weave cotton into garments, and now modern men are sewing coats, pants, and shoes in the modern world.

In this modern age of high science (technology), man's status of wearing good and beautiful garments, as the heavenly dwellers did in the beginning, has proven the need to be more sacred about going naked/nude. What this means is that man has reached the stage of being what Adam and Eve hiding from the public represents.

However, what Western societies have presented to the world is the reverse. Even though they have advanced human science to the point where they can make many different kinds of clothes, walking naked or half naked has been their culture.

Firstly, you see them (men and women) walking or lying naked or half-naked on the beaches or at the swimming pools. Let's look at the lady of the two old folks below:

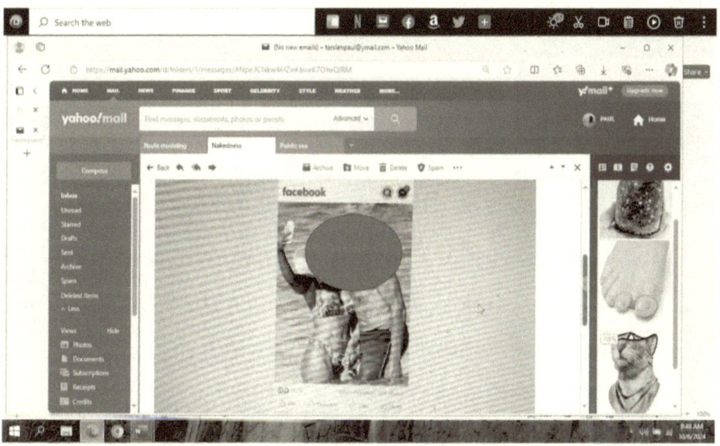

Secondly, they walk in the streets half naked, which is a woman wearing a G-string under a transparent lining.

Thirdly, are men's models wearing busters and women's models wearing panties on stage for a show of beauty?

For any Western reader, this may not mean anything to him/her because this is the life they are accustomed to, but I want to ask a few questions. (1) What code of dress do people identify sex workers with? (2) Why do sex workers dress in certain clothes, such as too short, too tight, or too transparent clothes? (3) How do women dress in bedrooms to entice their men, who may have been ignoring them or lacking sex interest? (4) What is the secret behind any woman dressing in her panties to work in front of her husband or boyfriend in the bedroom? Perhaps the golden question is, (5) Why are there laws restricting specific ways of dressing in workplaces, or are there terms like **decent** and **indecent** dressing?

After we have answered the five questions above, we can digest exactly what dressing naked or half naked in public, like the pictures shown in the link, should mean.

But I have two stories on this matter.

It was in November 2013 when I first visited the United States. I went to Miami Beach, and while I was walking with my brother-In-Law, who took me there for my book signing event, I saw the women and men lie down on the beach to catch the sun. Most men were wearing shorts, while most women were wearing panties.

I was so shocked to have seen husbands having their wives dressed that naked among other men. The worst shock came when I saw this beautiful girl with such a body that ticks me. On top of this, she was wearing a G-string that was buried into her buttocks, and when I saw that, I held on to my trousers, pulling them down every second to help me walk perfectly.

And while I was suffering in that condition, the Spirit of God descended on me and said to me, this is one of the reasons you were told that it would help if you came to the US to write the books you have been commanded
to write.

The Spirit of God then opened me up more to the seductive kingdom (Satan's other Kingdom of tickling human minds to desire sex more).
So, I learned a lot about its intrusiveness on those who desire more freedom to do whatever they want, and he said that's why they are more dominant in the Western world, from where they launch out into other cultures today so that gradually, every culture bends towards Western life.

In another story:
At age 17-19, I lived with my uncle in the year 1983-85 in Logan Town, Monrovia-Liberia. My after-school clothes were short pants and T-shirts.

My uncle worked, but his wife did not, so she and I stayed home almost throughout the day after my school hours as she sent me here and there, cooking and running errands.

One strange thing she did frequently while we performed cooking tasks in the kitchen together was to comment on my body hair: the ones grown on my legs and back, going down to my buttocks. She often told me always to keep my back covered with my shirt, and for the ones

on my legs, she quarreled with her husband, my uncle, for choosing short pants for me. She expressed her objection to him about my short pants, but he defended his reasons and did not buy long pants for me.

In the first two years, I did not ask her, but in the third year, I asked her why she disliked my clothes. At first, she dodged the question, but after a while, she opened up to me one afternoon. She said her husband had the same hair on his body, except I didn't have much on my chest that she usually played with while in bed.

Relentlessly, she burst open the secret of her heart to me on that happy afternoon. She said she was shy or afraid to tell her husband what she felt about my short pants, but the truth was that she used to see me all the time like her husband. She stopped short right there and ended with a question to me: "Do you think women have the same kind of feelings that men have about some women that makes them fall in love?"

I was shocked but understood what she was insinuating because I was also going through that same problem with one of my schoolgirls. The girl was slim, straight-walking, hairy, and had long lapping hair. My love for her was connected to her body look, so I translated her question to mean the same.

Given the matter under discussion, I believe everyone would agree with me that the reasons we lust after certain people have to do with something special about them, including the anatomies of those people.

Now, I don't want to write, but I shall lecture on the free flow of the spirit in an empty vacuum, which explains why everything (good and bad) flows freely in democracy.

So, democracy is the propellant behind people's renewing (bringing back) of nakedness.

Nakedness (nudity) was a life, not a choice, that ancient people lived out of necessity, not by genuine desire. Because they did not have clothes, they were still evolving. Their dislike of their living conditions propelled them to keep improving their clothing methods, and now we have better and more beautiful garments like the heavenly dwellers.

Democracy (by democracy, I mean its embodiment of

human rights teachings) has been exported from the Western world to every part of the world. In this Western cultural way of life, Human Rights promotion is a free ticket that permits everyone to freely do whatever he/she likes with few restrictions.

That is why nudity (nakedness) or half-nakedness receives rejuvenation in the corners of other parts of the world, including Africa, where there is this dance called "Mapouka" in the West African country of Ivory Coast. See this link: mapouka dance in ivory coast - Bing images.

Back to the '*Interpretation First*' book: You have been told about how our world received different ways of life called "Cultures and Traditions." In that news report from the Spirit world, I was given a diagram in that book, in which you will see how Satan posted other agents around the world as his ministers or local representatives, through whom he delivered his power to every corner of the earth.

These local representatives also instituted their own laws or ways of doing things, which were called "Municipal Laws." Under these laws, each agent of Satan introduced a specific lifestyle to his own people. This is why the world was divided into different kingdoms, each with its own language and ways of doing things, including the herbs used for healing and other things.

Another way of life for each kingdom was its style of singing and dancing, which constituted its way of celebrating festivities.

So, when the women came later, they posted themselves alongside these established kingdoms and peoples, thereby introducing their own women's laws and festivities along these men's already established systems, but in all their efforts to cajole men to fall prey to them, which is why these dances also exist in the Caribbean, Africa, and other parts of the world are all receiving rejuvenation through a Western system of human rights [every man is free to do anything he/she likes] promotion. These barbaric cultures were gradually going away at the advent of Christianity, but now they're receiving rejuvenation from human rights teachings [Freedom to do anything].

Suppose you went on YouTube to download this. In that case, you're going to watch women dancing with the playing of their tongues that [They are unaware] represents the snake world that controls seduction, even while they are seen touching and fingering themselves in public as the symbol of the power of the spiritual snake-like creature that cajoles any man that looks on.

However, it is a pity for the human world that thinks it is enjoying life, but behind the scenes are the powers that control these acts of ours, and these powers have some symbolic resemblances, such as when they are "Twerking" in that snake mood and while people dress in some Customs that bear horns or many eyes in celebrating some festivals.

We are victims of spirituality, but our hearts aid these forces, too, such as our desires. To better understand how our hearts aid the invisible world, God gave me the topic of ***The Information Superhighway,*** which I have drawn and explained in my other book, ***Interpretation First***.

Let me tell you something real. Things we take for granted in the physical world are dangerous moves by the Spiritual world. This happens because the Spiritual world that gave birth to our physical world remains the powering force of our world, which means that everything that happens in our world has already occurred in the Spiritual world, only ending in the physical world. But what happens in the Spiritual most often reaches the physical in an opposite or slightly opposite way. This opposite situation can best be explained from the point of dreams, which is why most people think that dreams are not real; instead, they're mere flashes of the mind on what one thinks about. Such a statement, though, is not consistent with all dreams. In some dreams, people go to places they have never gone to or thought about before or do things like flying with wings or swimming in the ocean they fear. This opposite condition of things is a true definition of Spirituality to Physicality, which means Spirituality predicts Physicality but in different forms at most times. Because I believe this, so I take every dream seriously.

Since I take my dreams seriously, look at what happened to me in December 2020

A Nissan sales agent made me buy a 2020 Rogue car without trading in my 2019 Sentra car.

I wrote to my legal firm for advice on taking him or the company to court. While I was awaiting the response, I had a dream in which I was attempting to climb up a ladder. When I got to the ladder to get my foot on the first step, one huge person who sat atop the ladder fell on me, and I was outweighed. Then I fell to the ground. END OF DREAM.

When I got up the next morning, I was sick inside my heart because I knew that something wrong was about to happen to my plans, but I did not know which of my plans since I had a few things planned in mind, including the Nissan case.

By the evening of that same day, I got my legal advice. It was not favorable. The attorney said I did not have certain proofs to back up the texts that I received from the sales agent about what he told me, which led to my following his advice. He also said that Nissan Motor Company was a big company that would delay the case in court, which would take several months or years before judgment was rendered, and as such, I would incur so many expenses for maintaining a lawyer.

Interpretation

For those who don't believe in dreams, this was just a dream, but for people like me who do, it has meaning.

1. **Failure:** Falling on the ground in the dream I knew represented a failure in something, but I never knew what that thing was.

2. **Something bigger than I am:** The huge person who outweighed me in that dream, I knew, meant that something bigger than I could take was going to outweigh me, and this became Nissan Motor Corporation in real life.

Manifestation

Among my plans, the plan to court Nissan company or its agent failed because the company is bigger than I am.

Hidden Beauty of Our World

The opposite between spirituality and physicality is evidenced by the dreams we often have, which are opposites of things we see in our dreams and how those dreams manifest in real life.

This is the same way things are happening in our human world that resembles God's Will but is not exactly what God wants. One such thing is democracy, and by democracy, we are talking about Capitalism since both work hand in hand.

Once again, let me remind readers that Western countries say their constitutions are primarily based on Christianity, symbolic of the Bible they use in their courtrooms. Therefore, God urged me to remind them of the Bible in every piece of writing I do.

Since we are talking about Christianity (the life and ways of Jesus), I hereby invoke the passage of scripture dealing with Jesus's life on earth. I don't want to use direct quotations here because everyone can recite them in seconds, but I will tell the stories.

[1] Jesus lived a life that did not involve trading. He called out those who were trading and told them to bring everything they had to the believers so that they could all share together.

[2] Jesus owned no personal property; he and his disciples owned everything together.

[3] Jesus beat those who traded in his father's house (The Temple, now the Church) because he did not want to deal in money. In fact, at one point, he said, "Give to Caesar what is Caesar," which meant that money was for the Kings of the earth and that he had no interest in the things of the earth.

Today, the world is confused about Christian life and government life because the Church failed to prosper independently but trusted itself to every nation's government. Thus, the government took over the Church, rendering it subject to the government.

This means that Jesus was establishing a different group of people who were to live independently from the government. They needed to develop their own system of growing food and doing everything together to avoid seeking individual material enrichment.

His example of how to live in this world was meant to

create an enclave within any nation. This "enclave" was going to be like what I knew in Africa as a "Mission Town," where Christians should live, and what in my hometown is called a "Country Town," where unbelievers should live. It was meant to rescue people from the country town (Unbelievers' dwelling place) to come to rest where there would have been no self-seeking of riches, thereby doing away with jealousy, envy, corruption, stealing, fighting, and killings.

His example of owning things together and working together inspired mankind to create a different government system. Let's keep going.

His calling of people from all works of life, such as calling Peter from fishing, where he was earning a living for himself and his family, and the calling of Levi (Matthew) from collecting taxes (A government job), was his way of discouraging people from pursuing earthly riches for themselves, which are the root causes of endless desires to own the whole world and to become insincere.

The government system that Jesus inspired is still with us on earth but has been corrupted to follow the one that the people had at the time—the system that sought individual gains was what Peter and Levi (Matthew) were part of before he called them.

The Kings owned wealth, and so did their ministers. The people in society all sought riches by marrying several wives and bearing many children, as well as owning cattle and more food. In the beginning, these were the measurements of man's wealth, and the people battered (Exchanged) them before the introduction of money. So, capitalism, herein referred to as an ownership system, existed but was not privatized.

Then came a new system of government called "democracy," which took some of the power from the King, now President, and distributed it in various forms we know today.

One of the distributions that democracy contains today is the privatization of wealth-seeking, now called "capitalism." It puts the way we should look for riches in the hands of traders/businesspeople to make most of the decisions, while the government or the King makes the laws to protect the traders'/businesspeople's decisions. That is why, from now on, I will always use the two terms interchangeably; I would say democracy when I mean capitalism or capitalism when I mean democracy.

The level of competition these two systems of operating the society brought upon mankind has led to people seeking more rights. One of such seeking rights is the one that originates from the women of the world, so there is a topic about the origin of women's rights in my other book titled *Interpretation First,* which brought about the preaching of "Human Rights or Everybody's Rights – the child's rights, the wife's rights" and other rights that are still popping up daily, along with all the business rights.

Therefore, democracy and capitalism have brought about a world order that God dislikes, but the human world celebrates because there is freedom to do anything you like with little curbs nowadays.

Life Under Democracy – The word democracy, defined as a form of government ruled by the people, is not about rule alone but is about all the components of capitalism and human rights practices. Since we will treat capitalism separately for some reasons, life under democracy is a subject of human rights implications.

As the people of the world keep jumping up in joy everywhere to receive democracy, the so-called freedom of the world, in Heaven, where God resides, there is so much hatred for the human world in which we live.

The reason is that God's hatred for Lucifer in Heaven began as soon as Lucifer sought freedom to do his own things. It means the desire to be free, as we call it, is a desire to deviate from God's laws.

Remember, when He made everything, He created laws that governed them. He set limitations to everything. He did not say to any angel that they were free to do their own things or to live whichever way they like, so Heaven is subject to Laws that require obedience to Him because He was the creator of all and had a purpose for every creation.

For example, you built your house and gave it to your son to take care of. You gave him laws on what to touch, how to touch them, and when to touch them because you know the purpose you made those things for, but that son of yours gets up any time of the day or night to do not according to your commands. What do you think will happen?

What will happen is distortedness and disorderliness.

That was exactly what happened in Heaven, leading to distortion (Misrepresentation of God, alteration of God's plans, falsification of God's name, and bias towards God's people). All of these led to disorderliness in God's creation system or ways of doing things.

As for bias towards God's people, my other book, *Interpretation Second,* tells us why human science is dispensed partially, which explains why one human race (white race) excelled more in science/technology than other races and why the black race is lagging behind all at worst.

So, the reason the world is like this is that two major different systems (God's ways to do things and Satan's ways to do things), which are subdivided individually into different denominations among God's own people, and different cultural systems and other systems among humankind is for the fact that Lucifer has desired self-freedom from God.

Consequently, what we celebrate on earth as freedom is not the kind of freedom God granted His angels, which was also purposed for man when He gave them Will-Power to choose among things that He had made available for them.

This freedom of choice that He freely gave them is like what we exercise when we go to a Buffet [self-serving restaurant] to buy food. Though we pay money at a buffet in our world, we are given the right to pick among the different kinds of food that are available there.

We are not cooking food for ourselves, but rather, the food is already made, and all we must do is to choose [make a choice] of what we want to eat. That is how Heaven is.

Unfortunately, Satan came into the picture, and there is this other heaven (it is called an "enclave" in the Heavens) where he resides. He is making photocopies of God's creations. He exacerbates/amplifies all that God had made in the beginning so that we now have different ways of love-making (The shoulder hold, the doggy type, the banging type, the 5-7 rounds or orgasm in a single night, even the cunnilingus or going down, which I call "lipping," and homosexuality) in addition to the way God wants love-making to be done.

See how we turned guns from hunting animals into killing our fellow human beings and see the different ways weapons of destruction are made today from ground to air and from solid to liquids – these are all evidence of distortion from the self-proclaim leader who is now the architect of the order of our days on earth.

So, do you still expect me to tell you who is behind the government system we cherish so much, who is behind capitalism, which enriches us most, or who is behind human rights teachings that are causing clashes between women and men, clashes among Christians, and nations around the world?

Can you now imagine where human rights teaching is heading our world when we see that people are so accessible to naked themselves [make themselves nude] anywhere?

Also, when we look at children quoting their rights in front of their parents- threatening to call the police on their parents for telling them not to do what they want, when we see women abandoning marriage to do it themselves, when we see men using themselves for a woman, when we see people using guns everywhere under human rights self-defense system, when we see the church breaking up due to support of government's policy of rights to practice any life even against the Bible, when we see that human rights have been prioritized over God's principles now when Christian government officials enact biblically abhorrent laws, when we see that the church has chosen human rights over the word of God now when clergy leaders themselves endorse the things under state laws that they have long preached against?

Now, let us reflect on the second impeachment trial of former US President Donald J. Trump on February 12, 2021, to see one of the ugliest sides of democracy: the misuse of freedom of speech—the right to say whatever you want.

Even though the then President of the US didn't stay out of the January 6, 2021 Capitol attack for what ordinary citizens could do, some Americans used democratic rights to justify Trump's behavior of support and cheers of that attack that almost took the lives of some Congress members and the then US Vice President, Mike Pence.

They showed videos upon videos of other US officials, who were not Presidents, who expressed opinions on criminal behaviors to justify Trump's right to say anything he likes even as a US Commander-In-Chief.

Senate Republicans refused to convict Trump by using two baseless arguments for not convicting him.

1. They said it was unconstitutional to impeach someone who was no longer a President, as in the case of Trump, but that was not true. Trump was impeached by the House on January 14, 2021, while still in office as President, while the Senate postponed its sitting for trial until February 8, 2021, after he had left office on January 20, 2021.

2. They searched histories to see an incidence of impeachment of any former president, which Trump was not at the time of the House impeachment. Yet, there was no one history of a sitting President inciting or launching an insurrection against his government in the US.

So, rather than being the first to write such history since the incident itself was the first in US history, they wasted all their time searching for records that were not in books. For personal reasons, they refused to seize the opportunity to be good history makers that future generations would refer to one day, given the peculiarity of Trump's actions.

Well, what the world witnessed on that Friday, February 12, 2021 from Trump's legal team was just the small beginning of what democracy is about to suffer. It was just the beginning of what God had told me to tell the world about democracy (The freedom to do anything), that democracy shall soon bite its owners just as God's granting of free will to the angels in Heaven did to Him, God, when Satan abused it by disobeying the laws of God, thus doing the wrong things to heavenly dwellers.

you see that men will soon begin to have women in public like the animals do while we pass by?

This is the impending danger that democratic societies pose right now when they cheer naked/nude models on stage like a lady in panties I watched the last time, and like the one I watched one time in which men models dressed in only briefs to showcase their anatomies. Let's see the below for women's modeling:

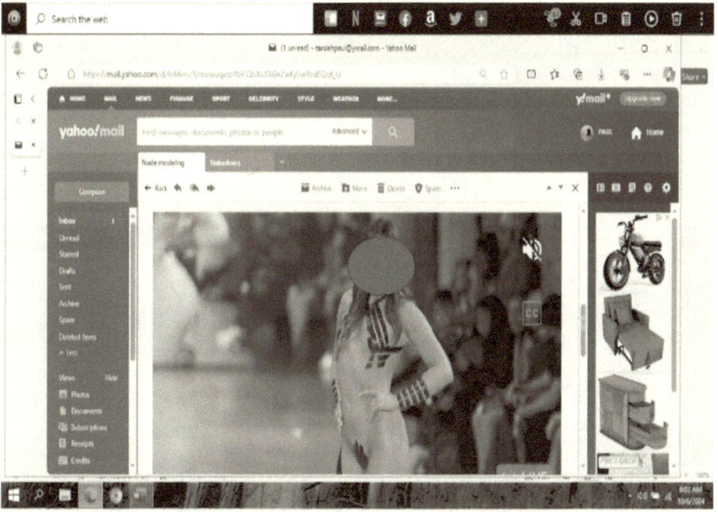

In fact, most recently, some ads have begun to appear on phones to advertise medications for men's ED. These ads depict sex videos of different styles that any underage child who handles a phone could view.

On Social media, there is a lot going on with explicit sex videos, and I wonder why they could be allowed on public platforms, where underage children go to see different activities. Oh, what a world of freedom to do anything!!!

Let's see the below:

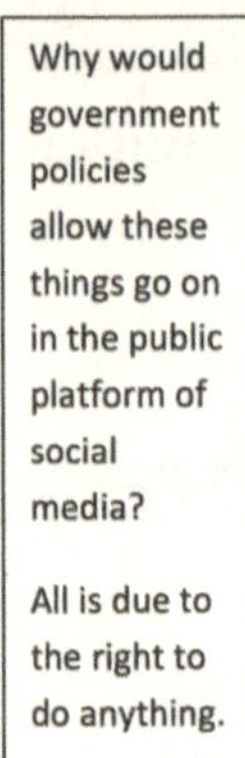

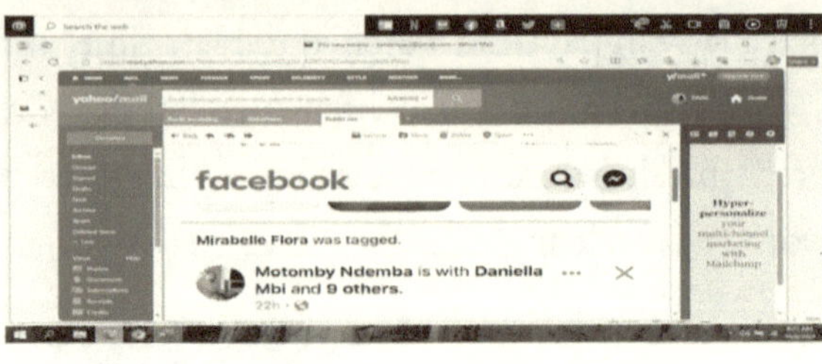

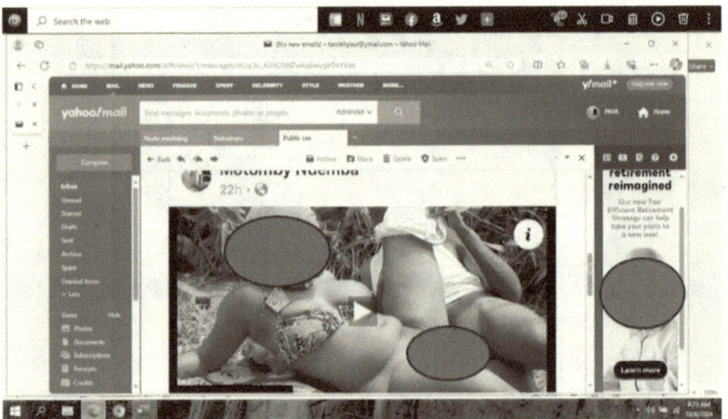

Listen, we're in the days of Sodom and Gomorrah, but we will soon enter the complete world of Sodom, where sex was done in the streets. It was the gravest event of the society that shortened the days of that generation.

So, democracy [government by and for the people to do anything] is the cause right now; let's celebrate it. At least, that's better to hear.

Life Under Capitalism

Living under capitalism is the unintended purpose of God, who did not create mankind to suffer such a life of self-struggle.

When Christ was about to leave the earth, he left his disciples with the Lord's Prayer. In that prayer, it is said that the disciples should pray and ask God for His Kingdom to come down so that those things done in Heaven shall be done on earth.

So, have Christians received an understanding of that prayer yet? Do they have clear knowledge of what Jesus said life in Heaven is?

Yes, Jesus told a little bit about life in Heaven. At one point, he said there was no suffering in Heaven. At another point, he said everything in Heaven was free. At another point, he said there was no buying and selling in Heaven. He also spoke about marriage. He also talked about housing in Heaven.

For this discussion, let us take "No suffering," "Everything is free," and "No buying and selling in Heaven."

Therefore, if Jesus told us to pray that God's Kingdom should come down one day so that the things done in Heaven shall be done on earth, then what was he referring to?

The answer is that Jesus was giving us a glimpse of what the New World that is to come would be like. It was to tell his followers and the would-be believers that the system they lived in, which has grown bigger in our times, was corrupt, counterfeit, or wrong for the world.

To address their temporary freedom of that system, he kept calling people out from that world of buying and selling to join him in forming a system for them to get away from that world of suffering. So, he introduced to them communal life, the life of doing everything together for the upkeep of all – No one owns anything, no one works for himself/herself alone, and more that should have come if they had followed his footsteps after he left them.

To discuss the three issues above, only one would summarize all, which is the "no buying and selling" issue.

In my other book, *Interpretation First*, I talked about the origin of money, which is a means of exchange in our human world today, but it is not any medium of exchange in Heaven. So, when Jesus said there is no buying and selling in Heaven, that should ring a bell in our ears, and that what we do with money on earth is not God's purpose. That is to say that capitalism, which we think is good for us, is not God's choice of the kind of life He preferred us to live as Christians – Christian country, Christian society, Christian people.

So, what do buying and selling do to our world? Buying and selling, which I'll now refer to as Ownership or Capitalism, is the root of all the troubles the world is faced with today.

The desire to own things for ourselves, not as a group, is the root of jealousy, envy, and the downtrodden, all of which birth to greed, cheating, stealing, lying, fighting, killings, and wars.

Now, let us look at a few words we are familiar with under capitalism to see their effects.

1. **Greed**—Google defines greed as "an Intense and selfish desire for something, especially wealth, power, or food."

Therefore, greed is the reason we experience price changes every day. Businesspeople concentrate on finding ways to make more money, adding a few cents or dollars to goods/services every day with different explanations about the changes. Take the example of the housing business in the US. Rental and mortgage costs change every one or two years, but wage rates remain constant for most people for many years.

2. **Lying** – Lying is making false statements or saying something untrue.

Because the world is driven by work-to-get-paid, people are forced to tell beautiful and harmless lies to their bosses just to keep their jobs. For example, no company's boss accepts certain excuses, such as being late due to attending to your child in the morning, so most parents would blame lateness on traffic and weather conditions or something that would sound well excusable.

3. **Cheating & Stealing**—Cheating and stealing are the practices of taking something that is not for you or that you feel is undeserving.

They are commonly practiced in workplaces everywhere, and several other terminologies, like embezzlement, soften the tone of the word "stealing" since the word 'stealing' may sound too harsh for a big guy in the company or agency.

These practices result from people's greed and their finding ways to increase what they get.

A recollection of myself: Before I came to the US, I did not think that corruption existed here since the US has always sung songs in my country and around the world about other leaders for corruption, but the Trump regime has made me know all about the works of the lobbyists, the millionaires who do not pay taxes or all taxes.

4. **Fighting, Killing & War** – Fighting herein refers to the daily struggle among people for economic survival. It also includes the pugnacity that comes with it.

When fighting heightens to pugnacity, it often degenerates into killing/murdering, often in the case of robbery.

The killings we see today through wars, whether by nations or individuals, are all for self-enrichment and are all forms of human practice around the world due to the desperate desires for wealth.

You can clearly see this struggle from the perspective of the US's patrols of the entire world and the accompanying wars they met on other nations to keep in charge - I mean the invasion of other nations to kill their citizens in all efforts to make them surrender to the wills and dreams of the Americans.

Here is an example:

After the G-7 meeting in June 2021, there was a news report that one of China's News Tabloids published a cartoon mocking Christianity and the West for their drafting a communique calling on China on several issues, including China's government's funding of Chinese businesses to help keep prices down on the global market, something that is to the disadvantage of Western companies that usually carry high prices.

At the end of the news commentary, the reporter hailed Christianity as the most successful movement in the world because Jesus said so.

The closing comment is what I want to highlight about what is going on now between democracy and communism.

I'll start by saying that Christianity has received mockery from the world population for a long time before China openly depicted it; it's not China that started it.

The mockery is just within the Christian nations themselves, where Western citizens are abandoning the Church's practices but leaning more toward secular activities, where people pass bills more on the things that go contrary to the very Bible, where capitalism [Focus on individual money making] is celebrated more than how the general masses could afford the luxury of science, where the printing of a new Bible is [Reportedly] emerging with a constitution enshrined in it, and so on.

Jesus is, but Christians shouldn't be, proud of the spread of Christianity all over the world because Jesus shall judge how Christian nations have used the Bible for their desire for the things of the world. [During my book tours, I'll be discussing the "Apocalypse" that Israel and the US/Westerners are using to continue wars in the world in which their Jesus called for an end to wars when he said, "No more of this."] Christian's "Apocalypse" is said to be God's destruction of the ruling powers of evil and raising of the righteous to life in a messianic kingdom." So, the US nation and Israel engage in wars to fulfill this prophecy, and that's why God wants to explain it better.

This is all to make more money from doing business (by selling goods—warplanes, commercial planes, and other goods and services) with the entire world and to obtain natural resources from those countries that would be used in the US to build the US's infrastructure.

So, capitalism (the game of money) is the root cause of wars and killings around the world, and the G-7 nations are bent on preserving it, even if it means joining forces to go to war against China. Yet, China's neighbors are blind to the fact that their region [Land area] shall be that battleground for the Europeans and the US.

This game of money, established under capitalism and spread to all parts of the world, is leading the world towards a period when some people will not be able to buy if they don't have enough money.

Look at what happened in February 2021 in Texas, USA, and the statement a city mayor gave to his citizens.

Please allow me to write an excerpt of what the news reported.

The headline was: **"Texas Mayor tells residents to fend for themselves during power outage: 'Only the strong will survive.'"**

According to the news, Texas mayor Tim Boyd told his citizens this on Facebook: "No one owes you or your family anything," a post deleted later, according to the KTXS AND KTAB OR KRBC news agencies. The news also quoted him as saying, "I'm sick and tired of people looking for a damn handout!"

The mayor's statement also described citizens as lazy residents who should find their own ways of procuring water and electricity. His statement immediately drew backlash.

Of greater importance for referencing the mayor's statement is Boyd's remark that he was 'sick and tired' of people looking for handouts and that the situation was 'a *product of socialist government*.'

For more information, click this link: https://www.bing.com/search?q=texas+mayor+tells+residents+to+fend+for+themselves&form=ANSPH1&refig=798457c5ee5d4071ae7af080bde33725&pc=U531

Boyd's statement that the citizens' request for assistance was a *style of socialist government* confirmed how capitalism has brought suffering and inequality to the world, that one group of people has abundance while others lack.

This game of money that is played around the world is clearly demonstrated under a system called "Stock Brokerage," in which individual persons put in money (Buy stocks) to get profit (Gain more money) in the far future.

People's desire to put [invest] their money in trading with business entities like Walmart, a grocery business, or AT&T, a service business, is a game of money (Recycling

Money) in the modern world that enjoys the pleasure of capitalism.

It is an economic system that makes costs higher before the future comes rather than working hard to reduce costs for more people to afford to purchase hands. So, it got capitalist economists working hard every day to increase costs, not cut costs.

Instead of economists working hard to bring down costs in the future so more people can afford life, their primary focus is increasing costs even before the future arrives. This is done when they calculate the current price of a thing and calculate how it should increase yearly so that in two/three/four, or ten years, how much the new price would be. It is called projection or future forecast, but this practice has no price reduction in mind except increases.

Citizens' or participants' eyes are fixed on nothing but making 'profits' every day, which keeps our societies in a continuous suffering mode with high costs for goods and services all the time so that the world is never going to experience low cost but higher cost forever and ever but with just a few people controlling enormous wealth in the larger sense.

5. **Jealousy & Envy** – Jealousy and envy are the desires to have what another person has or to look like the other person or nation.

These are reasons countries are going against one another. For example, they are reasons why individual persons in other countries, even in socialist/communist countries, would want to have more money like Americans do in their country. Americans also do not want other people to have more money than they, Americans, have. So, there is now a cycle of competition and conflict all around.

These two words show up clearly in Trump's administration. I mean, how can Trump himself [allegedly] take a loan from the Chinese government to invest that money in the US, but he gets angry over the Chinese people's booming economy? He seeks to bring down that country, saying they have more money than America and that it is their desire to overtake the US in the world. That is envy and jealousy.

He goes against Iran and North Korea, seeking to break down whatever they have as nuclear weapons because he believes the US is the only country that should possess them – saying that the US is the only country that should have them for peaceful use.

But it is the US that has ever used the most devastating (Atomic) weapon in the world and is still boasting of having more advanced types and is, under Trump, threatening to leverage any country to ground zero in the world if they don't submit themselves to the dreams and aspirations of the Trump America.

Therefore, I ask this question: Who is more dangerous, then—the one with more weapons to annihilate or the one still developing for defense purposes because he scares the big guy into coming easily?

6. **Downtrodden**—In Google, downtrodden is defined as "oppressed or treated badly by people in power." It is commonly understood as the practice of overlooking/con-

demning others because you have more power—always derived from having more money/properties, holding a top government position, or any other high-ranking position among the people.

Downtrodden is what every nation faces today under the US's hegemony of having more money and more technology that help to build its military equipment to use to subdue any nation.

As of the time of this book, the US's downtrodden attitude and continuous wars have invigorated a spread of wars and advanced science & technology among nations in the Asia region. See Russia improving its old Soviet-era weapons and acquiring new technology systems like drones and enemy tracking. See Arab fighters (Hamas, Hezbollah, etc) acquiring hypersonic missiles, drone technology, etc. See Iran's advanced weapon system used to break Israel's most boasted iron doom, Iran's satellite system to see into Israel and track US warships. See North Korea's advanced weapon system aiding Russia in the Russia-Ukraine war.

These are happening because the US and its Western allies wouldn't stop wars and downtrodden smaller nations. They have been using wars to invent new weapons every time and improving them each time they fight a war with any country, the same strategy Russia is using to advance its weapon system now beyond the capacity it had when Ukraine impeded them from their intended quick war without more casualties in the beginning.

To conclude this discussion on capitalism, I want to use my personal experiences to open a system-fix discussion on three economic activities in the US and other places.

1. **Loan system**

As a victim of loan deferment laws, I wish to see a fix to how people who lost their jobs due to protractive illness and other circumstances beyond their control, who do not have the chance of getting a job in no foreseeable time, could be protected and allowed to negotiate their future fate.

My point is that a lender could stop adding interest charges on a loan due to someone's health conditions or job loss based on circumstances beyond that person's control. I'll give you a specific instance during a book tour or discussion.

2. **Credit rating system**

Let me instantly cite my own case.

In December 2020, I completely paid off a loan to a company—$9,000.00 paid off at $6,000.00.

The company (anonymous for now) sent its report to the various credit bureaus, but the bureaus still maintained $3,065 ("Derogatory") on my credit report as of February 18, 2021.

The question now is, why should my credit be held down for months after I had paid off my debt? And why should the company that I owed and paid off have zero balance on their books, as reflected in their letter to me to confirm the payoff, while a different group of people still say that I have a balance due, which they use to hold down my credit score for months?

The most frustrating point is that my credit report was showing fair (650) in the system before they entered the $9K and a few dollars against me in November 2020, which brought my credit and my wife's credit down to unfavorable (550) positions. This happened to her because she was my guarantor during the purchase.

To fix our credit because we wanted to buy a house in 2021, I had to borrow $6,000.00 from our joint account. I was hoping to get a loan from the bank to replenish it as soon as my credit turned good after the pay-off, but here, my credit is still held down.

Consequently, I had to start paying extra money to Lexington Law Firm for my credit fix. In fact, Lexington Law Firm told me that apart from the specific issue that I was seeking a fix for, there were other negative points against me in the system that could negatively impact my chances of getting a loan or buying a house.

At this point, I got confused about what they were talking about, even though they promised to fix all of that. But did I really have to go through this process to get my credit fixed when I had already paid off my debt? How many people know about these negative points against their credit even when they have previously paid off other loans or credit cards?

They explained a lot about negative points against anyone with a deferred payment. Still, I saw all these complexities in the credit system as things imposed on citizens by businesspeople for their own benefit.

3. **Utility company's Contract system**

It is a system designed [unilaterally] to make a person enter into a year or half-year contract and be bound by it even when he/she loses his/her job. The person is also bound to continue payment even if that service is not good for him/her anymore, a system that the person wants to stop using.

Now, tell me how capitalism is good for the world. Isn't it that citizens are held captive by these business laws as the legal system is so complex and expensive to navigate by poor people [the majority in every society]? Since multinational enterprises know that ordinary people won't sue them because they won't be able to afford the legal costs, they take advantage of these things by imposing conditions on people, such as the credit score system, the utility system, the rent or mortgage system, etc.

A Look at Our World Under Communism

Communism is a form of government that seeks the ownership of everything by all the people. Before we go further, let us go to Google definition:

> Search: **What is communism in simple words?**
>
> **Meaning:** "*Communism* is a socio-economic political movement. Its goal is to set up a version of society where the factories and farms are shared by the people and would not have rulers or money." [Not edited since it's a direct quote.]

Do you see that? This was truly Communism's objective and is very much aligned with God's plan for how man should live in the world, but it missed its true desire when, at some point, those who started it decided to own properties for themselves, making it impure and short of God's standard.

In Heavens, the angels work but do not own anything for themselves. In Heaven, they share everything together; that's why they know everything God has taught them. Every angel in Heaven knows everything God has allowed them to know; that's why they rotate their works second by second, making every angel work efficiently and having lunch breaks all the time.

Their work in Heavens is done in short shifts: one comes, and one goes. This way of their coming and going is what we feel in our body system as the breathing system, or as the up-and-down movement of them that we call the air that enters us and leaves us.

Remember, the Bible reports that angels bring messages to earth and take messages back to Heaven. This process of their coming to earth to work and returning to Heaven to carry things has also been reported in my other book, *Interpretation First,* with more details.

This Communal living (laboring together) and social interaction (sharing friendship/love), called "Communism and Socialism," is what Jesus taught his disciples when he told everyone he called to bring what they had to the group for group sharing.

Jesus demonstrated the social aspect when they ate and drank together. Other things that they did together remain sacred.

He left the **communal** aspect (working on farms, building group homes, and developing their own technology) to the disciples to grow as a separate community within the larger community.

Oh my gosh, the man returned to his old ways.

The disciples (not the original twelve) returned to the same ownership system. They collected tithes and offerings from the people and began to live flamboyant lifestyles. They boasted all around as the men of God, and they forgot, maybe out of fear of persecution by state leadership, to develop themselves into an independent group within the larger group/society. They began to align themselves with state authority, and the state government became an influencing arm of the Christian body, which brought about a split among the people of God.

So, contrary to democracy that the earth celebrates/favors, Heaven loves Communism.

The amassing of wealth for the church or for individual persons in the church became a lucrative business. Now, there is no separate way to tell the true practice of the church from the state, and this has brought us to where we are today: the world is in chaos—everyone is talking about money, money, and money. We, as Christians, have missed the beautiful world, a hidden world of ours.

Communism is that world that we had rejected as a Christian nation. As a people who pride themselves on being for God, we should exist as an enclave (a separate community of believers) within every society/country.

Maybe the US nation should have adopted a communist system since the colony consisted of people from all over Europe and beyond who chose to live a separate lifestyle of their own. Then their country could have been the free land of believers to which people from all over the world would come by fleeing from suffering, but no, the kind of freedom people come for in the US, or they think they have in the US today, is not that Christian life. It is full of daily struggles for individual gains. It is the same life that Peter, Levi (Matthew), and the other disciples lived when Jesus called them to come to him for peace.

Communism could have been improved by now had it not been mixed with capitalistic activities, as we see in China and Russia today. These countries believe in the government having control of everything, but they also seek wealth for individual people.

That mixed-up system in Communism was introduced by other people's desires to own things for themselves, just as they saw people in neighboring societies do with democracy. So, democracy polluted Communism.

Now, in Communist/Socialist countries, there are two opposing ideas about how to do things. One sect always keeps the well-being of the people in mind, so the government thinks that the state must control everything. Another sect speaks to them to allow ownership of private businesses, too, so that people would have wealth like in other countries.

What did we [humanity] miss most?

Because we didn't embrace communism, we missed working fewer hours to have enough rest. We missed sharing science together so that everybody would be able to do the same kind of work, rest a few hours and go to the next department to fit one thing under the new car, sleep some more hours at home to go to the gym or buffet/restaurant, and rest some more hours to go clean the sewage for few seconds to let another person come to finish it. We missed a stress-free society in which people do not have to work eight or ten hours, only to earn less than required, so they must find other jobs to make up for the little they have. We missed a world in which robots have come to do the bulk of the job while we stay at home only to visit sites when needed for minor jobs, even while we get enough food to eat and have decent houses to stay in. We missed a world in which we did not have to pay taxes, rent, buy homes, buy cars, or use money for anything. Lastly, we missed a conflict-free world in which we wouldn't run competitions for everything. We do not have to steal someone's money or property or kill someone in an attempt to get what we envy or play jealousy/envy for because someone has what we don't; we do not have to fight wars to suppress others. After all, we fear they may surpass us and do many more things that we know are not good, but we do.

The Need for One-United-World-Country

Given the above, let me remind you of my other book, *Interpretation First*, in which I asked, "Why Can't Everybody Adopt a One-US World?" A one-US world that the United States of America should rule. But in that book, I didn't give a suggestion, so this time, my suggestion is that we have a *One-Unified World Country* by using this book to tell the world why it is important to start new discussions on doing so IF the US was not terrifying the globe by military postures and sanctions of strangulations.

In fact, I've seen that the world has already had the US land as the capital of the One-World-Country, not united yet, while all other countries are now serving as the US's states, and all their presidents are serving as governors of the US-led One-World-Country. However, this hasn't been officially recognized yet, which makes it essential for the world to begin the process IF the US is not scaring everyone.

How is it essential to our world today? It is crucial because of the little peace it will bring to humanity and the changes it will bring to the world. Look at it this way:

1. A ONE UNITED WORLD COUNTRY shall unite all the people of the world under one leadership that the US is already posing to by the presence of its offices in every country, giving money to those countries to solve their internal problems, and dictating how people in those countries should do things and live their lives.

2. A ONE UNITED WORLD COUNTRY shall remove walls, I mean borders system, remove economic competition among countries, and bring about universal road connectivity and development agenda so that the US and its Western allies shall use their technology and infrastructural development ideas to build every country just as they do for their states or cities. In this way, every area in the world shall be

well developed and universally habitable for everybody while creating more jobs, thus removing brain drains everywhere.

3. A ONE UNITED WORLD COUNTRY shall eliminate the notion of having an enemy and thereby eliminate the quest for wars and the manufacturing of weapons in general, thus reinvesting all the billions that go into military and weapons production in the building of infrastructure and human maintenance (Health care and education).

4. A ONE UNITED WORLD COUNTRY that creates more jobs and develops every part of the world equally, as it does throughout the states and cities of the US, UK, France, Germany, China, Japan, Russia, etc., shall end the mass movement of people from around the world who yearn to come to the US or the West alone for advance knowledge and for what they called "Greener Pastures."

5. A ONE UNITED WORLD COUNTRY shall allow the US to easily debate and sift through issues to take some good things from Communist China or Russia without fear that they're undemocratic. The same shall make it easier for Communist countries to accept the union of one democratic world country.

6. A ONE UNITED WORLD COUNTRY that accepts some communist policies, such as taking some powers from private businesses to support state funding of many things to reduce the high cost of living for everybody and also reduce individual workloads or hours of work before living a good life, shall pave a better way for the world to accept the deployment of robots to take over about 90% of man's work in this world.

Unknowingly to mankind, humans are the robots of the spirit beings to perform the complex tasks of what the Heavens need. So, by the time of this book's publication and the time of high human science, mankind is now performing about 75% of the labor that is required on earth, which makes it the reason the spirit world had sent me, author of this book, to explain capitalism and communism, in which to learn that human's deployment of the robot system is becoming difficult but necessary to do. It is for me to report that capitalism is a system that makes it difficult for the world to accept a full deployment of robots to take over man's jobs because capitalists cannot easily afford to let people work less or do nothing to get a good living. They cannot quickly develop a replacement system of work-to-get-money that would allow science to create more robots for mankind to stop doing hard labor in factories or offices or homes before they could earn wages to live their lives, but this is simple to adopt under communist thinking about the free living of people should these systems are brought together under a one united world country.

7. A ONE UNITED WORLD COUNTRY shall bring about many compromises, including better uses of technology. In contrast, censorship shall be acceptable in a general manner to curtail the wrong uses of technology, such as acts of hacking, scamming money, and the rest of what we know democratic policies make easy for technology manipulation.

8. A ONE UNITED WORLD COUNTRY shall bring about many more good things to eliminate many immoral acts among the world's people.

Why am I passionate about a One-United-World-Country? While the previous manuscript of this book was already undergoing content editing in January 2022, I started watching a Netflix series titled "Madam Secretary," but her name is "Elizabeth McCord," a retired CIA who became the Secretary of State after the death of the previous Secretary.

Of interest to me most is how Elizabeth continued to talk about America's interest in saving the world for future generations after she'd risked her going to Iran to pass on secret Intel to the Iranian regime that some powerful Americans wanted to stage a coup against by using some opposition Iranians inside Iran itself but without the official knowledge of the US government accordingly.

Elizabeth went to Iran without her husband's heartfelt approval, who feared that the coup plotters could kill her, and just as her husband's instincts told him, she narrowly survived the shooting that took place in the house of an

Iranian government official where Elizabeth went on a secret visit to pass the Intel to the Ayatollah's regime. One of Elizabeth's secret service officers was killed while lying on top of Elizabeth for her protection, and the host Iranian official was also killed in that incident.

During that house shooting, a young little boy who was the son of the killed Iranian official witnessed the shooting down of his father while Elizabeth was seeing him in the distance but called on the little child to stay on the ground from being hit by a bullet.

Unfortunately, that child could grow up with a grudge in mind and may choose to join an armed group to take revenge on Americans in blame for the death of his father or may direct his anger towards that Iranian faction that killed his father, and this would be how evil perpetuate through generations that no one or any nation can end.

My main point is that while watching the movie, even as I wrote this piece on January 22, 2022, I realized precisely how Americans have good intentions for the world but have the wrong approach to the world's problems. For example, Americans go to other nations to fight wars to get rid of those they call "Evils," but by killing human beings alone in those nations, Americans have also assumed evil status. They want to get rid of terrorists in the world. Still, by use of all those heavy artilleries and B-Bombers that blow out concrete buildings and kill people in mass numbers to suppress people in other countries, they also terrorize other people from whom come those who choose to express their grievances through killing sprees.

Let's digress here a bit. Can anyone tell why the US Capitol shooting took place to kill US Vice President Mike Pence? Let me tell you it. It happened as an expression of grievance. President Trump's supporters felt they were taken advantage of by those who didn't want to put him back in the seat of presidency anymore. So, they resorted to violence [underlined word is 'violence.'] It was an internal terrorism.

By sanctioning other countries, Americans also cause economic hardships for the masses of those nations, just as it affects all ordinary citizens of any sanctioned country. By going into secret business deals with other countries through means of lobbyists, Americans also engage in corruption they speak against in those nations. By running sex traffic like Jeffery Epstein, who secretly fed rich and powerful men with young girls for the satisfaction of their sexual desire, Americans are also guilty of the same crimes they speak against and call for persecution of people in other countries. By keeping technology a secret to themselves and alone from the world, Americans are stopping enough job creation worldwide, and more and more to list.

Therefore, I believe that the best approach to ending all these double games is for the world to have a One-United-World-Country to be ruled the same way the Americans do now but to unite every nation together while maintaining little autonomy for each to-be new province within the one-united-world-country, just as each US state under the confederate is, thereby removing all the conflicts in the world – grudges, envies, international wars, economic competition, developed and under-developed country differences, and to stop all the cries about who steals technology secrets and who owns technology, etc.

So, when you review the previous things I wrote about America and its Western lifestyles, consider them God's rebukes of the nation and its people's ways of doing wrong things, which mix up with their good intentions for humanity. And when you see that the Highest Spirit had sent down His rebukes through this book, then know that the evils in the land outweigh the good in the land, which is why the alternative that I suggest in this book about a one-united-world-country system should be a new discussion that America and the world should pick up now to fulfill Jesus's love-your-neighbor-as-yourself mandate issued to his followers and would-be followers before he left our human world.

Break Them, Restart Them

People are jumping up and down in the US, saying that they have the best system in the world. I want them to see a particular system that was developing in northern Africa that the US destroyed because the president of that country did not want to bow to capitalism.

This is the US's idea of breaking countries down to rebuild them with its money and thus with its admiration.

So, the world has been allowing the US to break down people's economies only to watch them start all over again, wherein they have to constantly look up to the West for financial assistance.

But it is not just breaking down nations; it is also breaking down other good systems that the US fears could undermine democratic systems. Because of this suppression of Communism, the world has not taken a good look at the goodness of Communism for a better world.

Now that COVID-19 has made the US ditch out free money to its citizens, which its people welcomed, I think it is time to tell the story of the Libyan people, where Communism was well-serving the people but needed more improvement had it been allowed to live on to now.

The Libyan module (Giving of free money) was a system that the US opposed being practiced for the improvement of the living conditions of Libyans.

So, the US chose to murder the president of that country who was trying so hard to change his people from following capitalism.

The Americans accused him of unfairly treating his people. They said he was a dictator.

Luckily, in April 2020, I read an article on Libya under the late Muammar Gaddafi. I found it more suited to explain the things God had told me to explain about Socialism/Communism.

Although, I lost the exact link to that news piece, you can still read ten good things about Gaddafi, including a few of the fifteen listed below, by using these links Ten Reasons Libya Under Gaddafi Was a Great Place to Live | The African Exponent and Never forget Libya: Under Muammar Gaddafi Libya was Africa's richest welfare state - The Herland Report (hannenabintuherland.com.

So, let us see how unfair (dictatorial) the president's policy was towards his citizens from the following excerpts (I inserted past tenses in brackets to indicate the change in time now):

Libya, North Africa under Gaddafi

1. There is [was] no electricity bill in Libya, electricity is [was] free for all its citizens.

2. There is [was] no interest on loans, banks in Libya are [were] state-owned, and loans given to all its citizens are [were] at a 0% interest by law.

3. Home is [was] considered a human right in Libya. Gaddafi vowed that his parents would not get a house until everyone in Libya had a home.

4. All newlyweds in Libya receive [received] $60,000 Dinars (US$50,000) from the government to buy their first apartment.

5. Education and medical treatments are [were] free in Libya. Before Gaddafi, only 25% of Libyans were literates. Today, the figure stands at 83%.

6. Libyans taking up farming as a career, received [used to receive] farmland, a farming house, equipment, seeds, and livestock to kick-start their farms – all for free.

7. If Libyans couldn't find the education or medical facilities they needed in Libya, the government funded them to go abroad for it.

8. In Gaddafi's Libya, if a Libyan buys [bought] a car, the government subsidized 50% of the price.

9. The price of petrol in Libya is [was] $0.14 per liter.

10. Libya has [had] no external debt, and its reserves amount [amounted] to $150 billion – now frozen globally.

11. If a Libyan is unable to get employment after graduation, the state would pay the average salary of the profession as if he or she is [was] employed until employment is [was] found.*

12. A portion of Libyan oil sales is [was] credited directly to the bank accounts of all Libyan citizens.

13. A mother who gave birth to a child under Gaddafi, received US $5,000 as child benefit upfront.

14. 40 loaves of bread in Libya costs [cost] $ 0.15

15. 25% of Libyans have a university degree.

Later, I went on the Internet to read more about Libya. I came across more information, of which I have the excerpt below in the box.

About Gaddafi, it reads: After coming to power, the RCC government took control of all petroleum companies operating in the country and initiated a process of directing funds toward providing education, health care, and housing for all. Despite the ineffective reform, public education in the country became free and primary education compulsory for both sexes. Medical care became available to the public at no cost, but providing housing for all was a task that the government was not able to complete.

Under Gaddafi, the country's per capita income rose to more than US$11,000, the fifth highest in Africa.

However, this increase in prosperity was not without its costs. Gaddafi's regime was marked by a controversial foreign policy and a rise in political repression at home, highlighting the complex nature of his rule.

As stated in the excerpt, everything was not perfect, but I can say that it was a working process. It could have been improved over the years IF there were not any foreign interferences, and what was termed "domestic repression" could not have existed or could have evaporated later as the people understood the system better.

To my own analysis, crises in Libya must have been fuelled by foreign countries, and the after result is a continuous civil war that is raging right now in that country, even as I write this line of this book on this Monday morning, January 4, 2021.

Author's Closing Word

I'm caught between what to say and what not to say, but I have the obligation to remind ourselves of the truth.

So, let me admit that this book, in large part, is about the US nation that has become the ruler of the world in everything and every decision-making, posing as the fixer of human dignity but is the very committer of what she thinks she could fix or make better such as the inspiring of regional conflicts, desiring of dangerous weapons, desiring of profitability (high pricing) over general affordability (low pricing), and so on.

Luckily, the world is waking up to the reality of things. Most of the world is evaluating the system as a new alliance called the BRICS bloc emerges to change the status of US-led practices and everything counterproductive to global development.

Nothing like the Taiwan Semiconductor Manufacturing

Corporation's (TSMC) style of moving its processing plant to the US can happen next time. It was the biggest mistake, with the potential of turning the entire world into a permanent high-cost environment for everything related to technology.

THE TRUTH IS that the world chose the wrong path for itself long ago by choosing capitalism over communism. Capitalism drives the world crazy towards excessive material gains, creating a great divide among people that we now call "haves and have-nots" in every nation today.

THE TRUTH IS that communism still thrives, so the world majority is now taking a good look back at it. This is happening now in the Global South nations. They're looking for an alternative means to develop their nations, so the China BRI system is gaining attention in the global south of developing and underdeveloped countries.

Communism was approaching its death path until recently when the US's excessive sanctions and tariffs with no limit hit two powerful nations, Russia and China. The no-limit action of the US and its Western allies has pushed these two technologically developed countries to turn their focus on the neglected part of our world, promising them what the Western bloc didn't do in those countries for centuries. China and Russia have begun helping the Global South Nations build infrastructures, develop technology growth, and rethink their market strategies.

Since these two Socialist nations embraced the capitalist system, they chose to reorient the market economy to benefit the world majority, infusing a socialist mindset with capitalist practices.

China is a strong socialist country that is committed to its socialist principles of caring for the social well-being of its people while partially embracing capitalistic practices. That's why they embraced the capitalist market rules to let their modern generations become a part of the wilder world.

It is under these rules that their young generations yearn for freedom to do things like people in democratic societies do - to live lives like people in democratic societies live, to own wealth like people in democratic societies own, to dress like people in democracy dress, to eat Burger and drink Starbucks coffee like democratic US's citizens do, to use the internet like people in democracy use it, to speak English language like people in democracy speak, to make love like those in democracy do, to go naked/nude like those in democracy walk as explained in this book.

Still, the Chinese government is facing challenges with how to play by the democratic rules, so they're constantly in conflict with the US and its allies of democratic nations.

The US and its allies want to eliminate socialism/communism from the face of the earth because it has a different version of what human freedom should be, which is why the Chinese use AI technology to monitor its citizens, just as God uses heavenly eyes [spying science] to monitor the angels from the time Lucifer rebelled against Him.

THE TRUTH IS that the world is drunk with the choice of excessive freedom of human behavior over curtailment of human excesses to create a peaceful world. Still, peace-loving nations wouldn't know this until the US succeeds in taking on China militarily to have communism fade out from the face of the earth completely.

I first thought this would happen if the US continued in the decoupling scenario to let China's economy crumble slowly because I thought this would force the Chinese to accept the remaining laws of capitalist principles, but since 2021, when I published the first version of this book, I have seen that decoupling can't destroy socialism; rather, it is strengthening the system to do more for the global world.

Decoupling is a peaceful means to resolve the China-US/West competition. Still, I don't see how the US/West would succeed without a disastrous military confrontation with China as long as the US/West is unwilling to compromise its profiteering strategy by borrowing the Communist style of state funding businesses to help reduce prices for the benefit of the masses.

So, the actual conflict socialism has with capitalism is that capitalism [Individual money-making system] is a game of self-interest-based practice that every nation has engaged in over its people's well-being. It prioritizes the continuing rise of the prices of goods. At the same time, the democratic government provides a fertile ground for businesspeople to continue to keep wages low all the time, which helps to continue perpetuating inequality throughout the world, unlike what the case would be if the people in socialism/communism had not abandoned the group-working-together and owning-everything-together system a long time ago. Still, it looks like socialists have just sought ways of improving theirs over the years, so they started to change capitalism/democracy by improving its methods. That is what the world is witnessing with China BRI (connecting the world through infrastructural development – roads, seaports and airports, technology development, etc.) It is the reverse of connecting the world through militarism (building and selling military equipment to teach how to destroy societies.)

Unfortunately, capitalism benefits a fraction of its citizens. For example, there is a large gap between wages and expenditures for every worker in today's world of capitalistic living. Imagine when minimum wages go up to $30 in the US [as a case scenario], the employers usually find ways to increase their prices of goods and services all the time, and that would still mean low wages for the poor because they get paid $30 instead of $15 but they still spend more for the same item that cost less in the $15 era.

In fact, I observed this tricky way businesspeople increased US citizens' costs in 2021. For example, last year, in 2020, I used to buy $30 gas to refill the tank of my Nissan Rogue 2020 car from Arco gas stations in Sacramento, but by November 2021, I could spend more than $40 to refill the same tank of the same car.

As I come to the end of my message from God, I want to tell us all that the democracy [freedom to choose what you like] we see today was once granted to the angels of the invisible world by God, but that freedom was abused and misused against the same God who created this freedom.

As the Bible has been preached to every corner of the

world by this time of this book, the story of how hardship came to mankind is not a piece of strange news anymore, even if we pretend not to acknowledge God's existence but the good thing is, God gave us his own story already to remind us that democracy that we're glamouring for is not going to end well for us, just as it did for the heavenly dwellers at the beginning of all things yet to come to a complete end.

Those who offered their opinions

My gratitude goes to Apostle Abraham Joe Kiamue and his five-man Committee members of the *Church of God Christian Ministry*, Monrovia, Liberia, West Africa. Thank you for believing in the Theocratic Ministry's work and dedicating your time to providing your reviews and comments for this book.

Also, thank you for accepting the role of a working partner to collaborate with the Theocratic ministry in recruiting its first team of entertainers who will help exalt our Lord Jesus through songs of praise while accompanying the Storyteller whenever he goes out on God's mission.

Commentary on the Interpretation Third

(Original edited, but content remains same)

The writer has used a lot of scriptures to point out that what he is saying is biblical. Therefore, before you say anything negative about this book, you might ask God to reveal whether what is written here is true or not. It happened to me (Apostle Abraham Joe Kiamue) the first time reading this book in your hand. It didn't make sense because I thought it was all about politics. But guess what happened? I dreamt and heard a loud voice, 'Read that book again.' As I woke up in the middle of the night, I picked up the book and read it page by page. My dear reader, I have fallen in love with this book and made it my companion from that moment until now.

In the introduction, the writer explains how science has turned everything God made to its glory. As the writer continued his history inside the book, he further said that most people in the Western world don't believe in the existence of God more than they believe in technology. Still, God would destroy the technology the scientists invented.

He also discusses many aspects of the Western world and compares Africa. The *Interpretation Third* is a road map to understanding the physical and spiritual worlds. I present this book as a key to unlocking what is lacking. Here, you and I can find undeniable knowledge.

Please meet these noble men and women of God.

1. **Apostle Abraham Joe Kiamue**

Apostle Kiamue, founder/general overseer of the Church of God Christian Ministry, born June 20, 1988, holds an AA degree in theology and several other diplomas and certificates in Biblical Studies.

2. **Pastor P. Eric Mandeh**

Pastor Eric, resident pastor and founding pastor of the Church of God Christian Ministry, was born on May 20, 1998, a high school graduate and obtained a "C" certificate in education.

3. **Min. Ophelia M. Vonyeegar**

Min. Ophelia, a choir director's assistant at the Church of God Christian Ministry, was born on March 18, 1990, and is a college dropout.

4. **Sis. Keturah Nahn**

Sis. Keturah Nahn was born on October 9, 1993, and obtained an AA degree in education and many other certificates in biblical studies. She is the children's ministry teacher at the Church of God Christian Ministry.

5. **Min. Annie Payway**

Min. Annie Payway, choir directress and head at the Church of God Christian Ministry, was born on March 24, 2004, and is still in high school.

Author's Biography

He was born to Jonah Seah Tarsleh and Elizabeth T. Jah on a farm in 1970.

He lost his father at the age of eight years when the father was assassinated with a gun, and the author was reared by his grandparents in a town called "Putuken" in River Gee County, Liberia, West Africa.

He's been a Christian and a Baptist by faith since he was a teen. Still, he was baptized in the Church of Christ in 1997 after he received the first conviction that he needed to do the right thing during one of their evangelical teaching tours to him while in the hospital with his sick son, now deceased.

But why did it take him so long to get baptized? Well, that was because when he first started attending church, he went with his grandpa, who was a Baptist and with whom he had an amicable relationship more than his grandma, who was a Pentecostal member.

He had so many questions about being a Christian since

all the people were still doing the things they were preaching against [adultery, fornication, promiscuity, polygamy, drunkenness, lying, gossiping, consultation with the devil, and all the likes], including pastors who went in bed with church members.

At most times, when he heard his friends jumping here and there for the joy of going to choir practices or going to church conferences, he asked them whether it was for the girls in the choir department or those in the congregation whom they were having time with and talked about all the time that they were serving God for, or that was their major purpose of being a Christian, or there were some other secrets about serving God.

This same purpose of questioning Christian life [seeing them doing the things that they preached against] had made him cancel his first baptism, which should have been done as early as 1985 in the Providence Baptist Church, the first and biggest Baptist Church in Monrovia, Liberia, West Africa, after attending two weeks of baptismal classes in January of that year.

Even after baptizing in the Church of Christ in Abidjan, Ivory Coast, West Africa, he still discovered faults among them that were contrary to what they preached as the pillar of their doctrine.

So, instead of remaining in their Church as he previously thought, he returned to his Effort Baptist Church in Tabou, Ivory Coast, where he served as a general Secretary in 2004 under the caretaking administration of Bro. Robert Teally after Pastor Freeman had left for Abidjan for the UN's Resettlement program.

After returning to Liberia in 2006, he served as a Bookkeeper in 2008 for the Messiah Mission Church School in Monrovia, Liberia.

While serving as a bookkeeper, he taught English from grade seven to nine, served as a member of the Church's Men's department, and was honored as Father of the Year in 2008, for which he received a certificate.

As for his educational background, he is a high school graduate who served as valedictorian in 1989 for his graduating class and thus obtained a government scholarship to go to university the following year, 1990, where he wanted to do Mass Communication and Political Science, but Civil war broke out in that country, and it took his opportunity away.

To this date, his highest level of education is an 18-month vocational study in Bookkeeping and computer literacy.

Once again, misfortune came in—misfortune is his human word—when he set out to acquire more knowledge of the Bible in January 2006 when he registered for a two-year evangelical study at the "Maranatha Evangelical School" organized by the Tabou-Liberian Assembly of God Church, but something mysteriously happened to him on the night that he returned from his first class.

On that night, he was lifted from bed while he was asleep. At first, he was in deep sleep when he noticed himself being snatched out of his bed, just as is in a dream when you seem to be flying, going up like a rocket plane. Still, when he opened his eyes in fear, he saw two hands slipping off his two hands, and to his surprise, he was suspended in the low ceiling of the apartment room that he rented for 40,000

CFA. He came down to the ground just when his fiancé jumped up in wails and grabbed his waist.

Hallelujah. This is the day he was changed from what he was before this incident to what he is now as a new person with a spiritual body.

Why was he lifted?

According to the spirit of Christ, this lifting was allowed by the good forces of God, acting on the mandate of God, to give him a practical understanding of how Jesus was lifted from the grave. It was also meant to provide him with practical knowledge of how the rapture and the resurrection shall be when the end comes. The instant change of his body was meant to help him understand and teach how the righteous shall instantly become new people, having new bodies, and, in their case, they shall not know the old things again.

Even from that day, he began to carry within him certain powers that manifest each day to guide him in some things, including writing all his books.

A few months after receiving the Spirit of Christ, he was made to understand that he had experienced a power encounter on that night when the evil forces came for him to prevent him from going to study the word of God since this would have made him more resilient against the evil practices in the world. Still, then the Spirit of Christ [An Angel] came down from heaven right away and rescued him from those hands that were taking him to an unknown destination.

Now, when the angel of Christ had rescued him, he said the incident didn't only take him to the Kingdom of Darkness, but it exposed him to that world in a way that qualified him to speak the things that he knows in the dark world and the things that the Light world shall pass on to him in the years to come. So, for two and half years (2006-mid2008), he kept under the voices of the people of light (the spirits of God that delight in good things). The result has been the books he has been writing based on his spiritual impartation, each of which deals with one major topic based on the Holy Bible while touching on other aspects of our living conditions from the world around us.

During the two-and-a-half-year period mentioned above, he was labeled by his people as insane or mentally deranged since he was doing and saying things out of the ordinary.

Today, he can say they were right because he took on the body of a man who communes with the unseen forces. In this state, he could see invisible things that anyone sitting by him couldn't see. He could hear what anyone sitting by him couldn't hear. In this same state, he bought a hardback notebook in which he took notes and made drawings of diagrams like the one depicting God in His trinity and the one describing what the spirit gave him as "The Information Super Highway" that is meant to explain how our communications from the heart (Those very secret things of the heart that people around us cannot hear or see) trigger the spirit world into actions that define who we are. He still has that notebook.

While he was doing all this, he kept telling them that he was taking notes from the spirits who were telling him that he was going to write these things into books for the world and that he was going to leave Africa to go to the Western World, where he would be able to explain all of what he was taking notes on.

All of these made no sense to his people, especially when he said he would go to America, which was the worst utterance out of human imagination since he didn't have a job, and even if he had one, how much would have been his salary at that time in Liberia that could have given him the amount it costs to pay for a plane ticket. Yet he told them that the books were going to grant him a US visa and that he didn't know how he would have gotten the money to travel, but one sure thing is that the spirits kept telling him that the time was yet to come for him to get the money, so he needed not to worry over that.

Indeed, in the middle of 2008, he received a message from the spirit world saying that he had now graduated from the theocratic school of the spirit and was free to go into the world to do what everyone does by finding work to do.

So, he set out, and he got hired by a friend to teach in his computer school. Then, after three months, he got called by the Overseer, Rev. Gballah, of the Messiah Mission Institute, to come audit his school's financial books since he was not getting a clear picture of what was happening in his school. He conducted the audit and was paid $3,000.00 Liberia Dollars @ a rate of 60:1, which was about $50.00 US dollars.

Based on his recommendations, the Church overseer found no one qualified to implement them; therefore, the overseer chose to hire him as a bookkeeper next to the school's female accountant.

The author was too strict and caused others too much embarrassment, so something happened, and he had to resign.

In 2009, he took another Bookkeeping job at the

Cuttington University Credit Union in Gbarnga, Bong County, Central Liberia. In December 2010, he took employment at a multimillion-dollar Iron Ore mining company, ArcelorMittal-Liberia, as a Procurement Officer (Buyer), where he worked until August 2014, when he left to visit the US on a leave break but didn't return to Liberia due to the Ebola outbreak that year.

How he made enough money to publish his first two books with AuthorHouse, UK, in 2013 and 2014 and raise other money to travel to the US is one case scenario meant to explain "Imposed sin," which is out of discussion now for others' privacy.

And precisely as the spirit had earlier predicted through him, that's how he came to the United States for the first time in November 2013. This means he obtained his US visa in 2013 at the invitation of AuthorHouse, UK, to participate in a Book Signing event for his two books in Miami, Florida, USA, that year.

The job that brought him money, receiving a US visa without delay, and traveling to the US, all served as the first fulfillment of the things the spirits conferred on him and predicted through him. They've been his initial strengths and are why he believes he has a genuine mission to fulfill. That mission has just begun, for the world has a lot to hear yet, but it will be made possible by those who read this book and all of his books, whose purchases and other supports shall make the mission more fulfilling.

As you're set to read this book, he wants you to know that he's doing the unconventional thing (revealing materials more than written in the Bible) because he's just a storyteller, not a biblical writer. For this reason, he didn't quote Bible verses at every point where he referred to a biblical matter; rather, he explained the issue like he would tell any other story.

However, there are several areas in which he endeavored so hard to provide scriptures just to become conventional but not necessarily crucial according to his duty.

About the Author

He is a Liberian writer who was born in 1970. He came to the US in 2014 and has published three books there, with this one being his fourth.

He graduated from High School as a student journalist. Still, his interest in writing was enhanced by a mysterious power that took over his body in 2006 when he began to hear voices in his ears and breathe out exhaustively. Such voices and powers told him many stories about our human world and thus commanded him to write many books that blend religion and every field of work together.

This book, Interpretation Third, is one product of the inspirations he received during the two-and-a-half years from 2006 to mid-2008.

A dark period in his life that he described as Domination Time was when those voices told him stories of the US nation and its place in the world of nations. So, this book is not entirely his imagination but a combination of what he learned from those unseen people and what he knows about the US and the world.

A caution from him to everyone is that the world needs to develop a different module for Africa because Africa is coming last in receiving development but should not be used the same way every other continent has been. This is a special message from those we don't see but have authority over everything happening in the world. This is one big message that the author comes to tell the world quickly before D-Day comes for all. So, this book and the other title, "The Interpretation Fourth," are meant to allow him to speak to America and the developed world about what is due them.

www.ingramcontent.com/pod-product-compliance
Lightning Source LLC
LaVergne TN
LVHW041212150826
845673LV00001B/376

* 9 7 9 8 8 9 5 6 9 7 8 8 7 *